SMARTY JONES

FOREVER A CHAMPION

BILLY VALENTINE
WITH TEAM SMARTY

BRAVEHEART PRESS, LLC
MALIBU, CA - WASHINGTON, DC - FLORENCE, OR

Books by Braveheart Press may be purchased for educational, business, or sales promotional use. For information please write: Special Markets Department, Braveheart Press, LLC, 23852 Pacific Coast Highway, Suite 572, Malibu, CA 90265.

First Edition

Front Cover Photo by Jeff Coady. www.coadyphoto.com
Front Cover Design by Raine Ruffin
Back Cover Photo by Equi-photo, Inc. (Bill Denver) www.equiphoto.com
Back Cover Design by Lucy Nicolosi
Insert Photos (1-11, 16) by Jeff Coady, (12-15) by Kim Pratt.
Photo Insert Design by Mrs. Estherhaus
Library of Congress Cataloging-in-Publication Data - Pending.
ISBN 0-9763935-1-4

*This book is dedicated
with deepest love and affection
to my daughter, Alison.*

*May all that I do
in the remainder of this life assist
in your understanding of how
loved you are, how you have
inspired me, and how greatly I
value your respect.*

ACKNOWLEDGEMENTS

THANK YOU to everyone who has had a hand in the bringing forward and completion of this project.

I am quite certain that I will forget more than a few of those who have impacted me either directly or indirectly in ways that have resulted in being at the life station which I currently occupy. However, should I fail to appropriately honor anyone at this time, there will most assuredly be another work which will afford me time to adequately reflect on the names I have been unable to recall at present.

I thank My God for the gift of life, family, reasonable intellect, the ability to feel and express those feelings in thought and word. I thank my family for their love and understanding.

I thank Roy and Pat Chapman, and The Servis Family, Stewart Elliott, Bill Foster, Maureen Donnelly, Pete Van Trump, Mario Arriaga, and of course, the MAGNIFICENT "Smarty Jones," who is not just "Forever a Champion," but also forever an inspiration, forever a prankster, forever a hero, and forever my friend.

I thank those who have always known that I could succeed, as well as all those who were equally confident of my perpetual failure. You have each inspired me in ways in which only your respective attitudes could insure.

I thank my Aunt Edna and my Grandmom Bess for saving me from certain death at the hands of my father. If your efforts on my behalf result in one person laughing, crying, smiling, or feeling any-thing from the manner in which I write, those efforts will have had purpose.

I thank those involved in the thoroughbred racing industry who have assisted me in obtaining a more significant knowledge and understanding of this business. Specifically, in this regard, I thank Frank McDonnell, Joe Wilson, Kim Pratt, Lance Morrell, and the rest of the Executive and Administrative Staff at Philadelphia Park. I thank C.J. Cella, Owner of the Oaklawn Jockey Club in Hot Springs, Arkansas. I thank Nick Zito, Mary Lou Whitney and John Hendrickson. I thank George Isaacs and Milton Hendry. I thank Dr. Patti Hogan and the staff at the New Jersey Equine Center. I thank Jeff Coady, Steve Haskin, and Laura Hillenbrand.

I thank Dianne Frye for the natural love and affection which few in this world ever enjoy. You have always been there for me in one form or fashion and will be there in the future, also. I also thank David Frye, if for no other reason...he's a really cool guy. I love you guys.

I thank Lucien Hold, Buddy Bolton, Peter Rosegarten, Merv Griffin, Tony Rock, Sherrod Small, Paul Sears, Beth, Ken Tanana, Chris & Stephanie Pantas, Diana Redmon, Caryn Swanson, Nancy Chiffens and Denise Salopek.

I thank the extremely lovely Regina Hamner, Chris, Alice and the rest of the staff at Atlas Books. I also thank the incredibly talented Bill Cosen, Tim Fleming, my best friends Raine and Charlie Ruffin and the rest of the people at Braveheart Press.

I thank Joe Suba, Greg Niemczyk, Ken Stohs, Ted Power, Paul Klipowicz, Steve Anson, Rex Christner, Dave Tuttle, The Late Phil Wilson, Roger

Schmuck, Floyd Bannister, Ray Torphy, Rich Harold, Tom Tarka, Laverne Morrissey, Pat Sicilia, the Wacker Brothers, Paul Barkley, and John & Mouse Duffy.

I thank Adj and Tim for understanding why this one is for Ali. I love you guys with every fiber of my being. I thank Lorraine and Dane for taking great care of Ian. Your dad loves you, Ian.

I thank Frances Torpy for friendship, fellowship and spiritual guidance which I know will always be there. You're the greatest.

I thank Stanley Basgall, Kevin Kuhn, Mike Hanson, Rich Pennington, Harold S. Bauduit, Tom Mellon, William "Billy" Keenist, Len Pasquarelli, Phil and Lundi Denfeld, Larry Klar, Pat Smythe, Garry Zimmerman, Russell Valentine, Big Daddy Graham, Don Imus, Katie Couric, Steven R. Zieber, Bob Tilton, Billy and Bryan Wilkinson, Anne Marie Wilkinson, Terry Beck, William F. Keller, Freddie Keller, Susan Smith, Keely Solem, Lushington Thorogood, III, Charlies Siropadis, Pilar Siegrist, Donald Thomas, Cheryl Gohde, Cliff Hubbard, Martin Knoblauch, Andy Geddes, Ron Mullay, Jim Concannon, Carl Monk and the Late John Howe.

I thank my Mother, my Uncle Jack, and my Great Grandmother, the confidence in my faith allows me to know that you are not only witnessing this entire effort, but overseeing it, also. I thank my lifetime friends Cris, Emilio, Pasquale and Maria, Tina and Rob, Rosie and Jerry, Bob and Kathy, Susie Flood (especially for finding the Quark Expert), the worldewide community of Smarty Jones Fans, and the all inclusive EVERYONE ELSE who KNOWS I should have thanked them. Please forgive the combination of absent-mindedness, and or a mentally defective condition which left you out of this work.

As I mentioned above, there will be other works, and I WILL remember you all.

TABLE OF CONTENTS

Smarty Jones

Forever a Champion

Billy Valentine
with Team Smarty

CHAPTER ONE

FIRST IMPRESSIONS

IT'S A BOY!

Like most of us, Deb Given had been over the course of her adult life, routinely asked if she could remember where she was when a President was shot...or when the Berlin Wall came crashing down, or when some other life-changing or world-altering event had taken place. Until recently however, she had never once been asked, "Where were you, on February 28, 2001, at 9:05 PM?"

This too, while not, *"a day that will live in infamy"*...was a day that would change her life, as well as the lives of anyone who would later be touched in some way by one of the most popular and beloved sports heroes of this, or any age.

For you see, on February 28, 2001, at 9:05 PM ...Deb Given, with a firm grasp on the front legs of a slightly undersized chestnut foal, still partially encased in the womb of a mare by the name of "I'll Get Along," single-handedly delivered, and welcomed Smarty Jones, not just into this world, but into the heart and soul of an entire generation, as well.

Deb Given was the Barn Manager at Someday Farm, and had been a loyal and trusted friend of the Farms' owners, Roy and Pat Chapman, for nearly nine years. She had also been the closest thing to a friend, that you could say about anyone who had ever come in contact with the mare now lying on its' side in front of her...and even Deb had been "caught pretty good more than once" by that same horse's hoof when the horse didn't especially like where she was standing, what she was doing, what she was saying, or even what color socks she happened to wear to work on any particular morning.

I'll Get Along had a tendency to kick, and kick HARD! It mattered little who you were. Even if you were there to give her a bath, fill the food tray, offer a kind word, or just admire her for her earthly beauty...if you were within striking distance, for some reason it was important for her to make sure that you knew that she knew she could reach out and touch you at her whim or folly.

How much this "attitude" had to do with Trainer, Bob Camac's suggestion that the Chapmans breed her to a horse named Elusive Quality, we may never know. However, those closest to the process, and who would one day have to care for the offspring, were about thirty seconds away from holding a candlelight vigil and praying that the horse was slightly less nasty than its' mother.

Bob Camac was, by everyone's account "a quiet man." He had been in the horse business all of his life, and it WAS his life. He was a Trainer who came to work, did his job, spent literally every waking hour studying horses; and as a result, was someone a horse owner listened to when he suggested that a breeding combination be considered.

Bob also loved sprinters. They were his true passion within the racing industry...and when he spoke to the Chapmans about breeding their mare, I'll Get Along, to a powerful stud horse named Elusive Quality, for $10,000.00; they took his advice.

In this case, however, Bob Camac was walking Roy and Pat Chapman out onto a potentially very long limb. Elusive Quality was a brand new Sire in 2000. He was not only unproven, but virtually untested as a thoroughbred king maker, in every way. Roy, who most people simply refer to as "Chappy," wasn't worried, however. "I've rolled the dice more than once in my life for that kind of money, and on lesser confidence that I had in Bob," he pronounced.

Chappy is a very interesting person. A real battler in every respect, his competitive instincts and resolve are paramount in all that he does in sports and in life. He is one of those people you meet in life that you know right away is going to be either "for you, or against you" and you will respect him and his decision, either way. You also know immediately that it would be a much better thing to have him, "for you."

Chappy was FOR Bob Camac. Their relationship was built of mutual respect as horsemen...and more importantly, as men. "He (Bob) didn't care about money, or fame, or anything," Chappy related. "Sometimes he'd go for months and months without ever even sending us a bill...and he had all of our horses." "He just loved horses...no better horseman in the business, I'm telling you," according to Chappy. "When it came to breeding, what Bob said, was the way it was going to be."

I'll Get Along had been sired by a horse named Smile; by anyone's account one of the greatest sprinters in the history of the sport. She was a big horse, 16.2 hands, to be exact. Elusive Quality was also something of a giant, standing the same 16.2 hands in his own right. Together, they would most assuredly produce what is known in racing as, "a monster"...a racehorse that enters a track and turns every head, including those of the other horses in a race, who all of a sudden decide that they don't feel so good and want their mommies to let them stay home, from what will undoubtedly be "school" that day.

During the delivery process however, Deb Given would note that Smarty Jones was a full twenty percent smaller than his pedigree would suggest. "He was surprisingly small," Deb said. "Very surprising, because his mother was simply huge." At Bridlewood Farm, in Ocala, Florida, where he would be broken and turned into a race horse, those closest to him would refer to Smarty Jones as "a runt"...and when Maureen Donnelly, Assistant Trainer at the John Servis Stable, would see him for the first time, she remarked that the horse was "something of a shrimp."

Almost from his first breath however, there was something more than a little bit "special" about Smarty Jones. Perhaps the very first special event, was Smarty's birth, in and of itself. "It was very cold that night...bitter cold," according to Deb. "But once he started to come, there was pretty much no stopping him."

The birth of this horse has been talked about, written about, chronicled in songs from rap to country...and described by the only human in attendance, as "an easy delivery"...so routine that the only veterinary medical involvement was a postpartum phone call to let the good Doctor know that all was well. Not so, for at least a dozen of Smarty's half siblings, and over five hundred thoroughbred foals conceived in the Class of 2001.

Beginning in that year, virtually the entire

thoroughbred breeding community in the Commonwealth of Kentucky was struck with an illness which would ultimately come to be known as "Mare Reproductive Loss Syndrome," or "MRLS." While no exact cause has been determined, contemporary veterinary medical science suggests that caterpillars, who had eaten leaves off of black cherry trees which contain cyanide, were later eaten by mares in foal, transferring the poison to the foals, resulting in stillbirth.

It has been reported that sixteen, of the fifty-five mares who were bred to Elusive Quality in 2001, produced offspring which were stillborn; many, if not all, as the result of MRLS. All five hundred deaths, including those involving mares bred to Smarty's Sire, occurred in Kentucky.

From almost the moment the two entered the sport of thoroughbred horseracing, Roy and Pat Chapman had a dream...to one day take a Pennsylvania Bred horse to the Kentucky Derby... and bring home a trophy for their mantel. The only way they could do exactly that, would be to either find a Pennsylvania Stud to mate with their Pennsylvania Mare...OR, take their Pennsylvania Mare to Kentucky for mating, but return soon enough thereafter, so that the offspring would still be considered a Pennsylvania Bred. With Bob Camac's assistance and guidance, they chose the latter course. I'll Get Along was transported to Kentucky for breeding and then returned to Someday Farm, in Chester County, Pennsylvania almost immediately after. As the result, I'll Get Along wasn't IN Kentucky long enough to be impacted by the disease, or transfer it on to Smarty Jones. I'll Get Along spent her entire time in foal at Someday Farm, in Southeastern Pennsylvania where there were no black cherry trees...and no reported cases of stillbirth due to MRLS.

Already, it seemed as though this horse had been touched by some higher power, perhaps destined for greatness...and Smarty Jones wasted little time in grabbing the gift of life and running with it...always at full speed.

Very young horses tend to be curious; but for the most part more skittish, than curious. They want to know...but they don't want to know; especially if it scares them to find out.

Smarty Jones was afraid of nothing. The Staff at Someday Farm remember Smarty as "an in your face kind of horse," who wanted to know everything. This was, of course, not to say that he wanted to face each and every new life encounter, on his own. In the same way in which a duck will imprint upon a barn cat, and follow it as though it was its' mother, Smarty decided, literally within days of his birth that wherever Deb Given would go, the lamb; or in this case, the horse, was sure to follow.

As thoroughbred racehorses go, Smarty may have been small; but then maybe he wasn't REALLY a horse, after all. It certainly seemed to everyone at Someday Farm, that Smarty Jones was, in reality, a four year old boy, trapped in a thoroughbred's body.

Oh sure, he picked up his birthmother's kicking habit...but, he never once tried to hurt anyone. "His momma wanted to hurt you," Deb remembered. "She was just a nasty horse." Smarty, on the other hand, he kicked at his stall, just hard enough to let you know that he knew Deb needed his "help" with whatever she was doing on the other side of the farm. Then, when he was let out and finally caught up with his adopted mommy...he would kick at her, playfully; like the four year old who pokes repeatedly at his sister while saying, "I'm not touching you...I'm not touching you...I'm not touching you." At other times, he would tap Deb, and then run, as if he expected her to chase him; and when she didn't...he would come back to her and nuzzle until she gave him pets. "You just had to love Smarty, from the minute he arrived," she said. "He was a real prankster, but a joy to be around, from the word go."

On Sunday, the only day that Deb Given ever spent away from the farm, Smarty wasted no time in imposing his good-natured torture tactics on her replacement, Melissa Coring. "He was a goof," according to Melissa. "He would knock over buckets, and then smile at you...or take keys out of your pocket, and not really throw them, but just drop them at your side...almost like he was saying, I gotcha again!" And whenever he was chastised, he looked and acted as if he knew exactly what was being said; why it was being said...and once again, he cared about as much as any other four year old

8

little boy...or six month old little horse.

"I've been around horses all my life," Deb told me, "each one has their own very distinct personality." "Smarty...from the night that he was born, he wasn't like any other horse I had ever worked with. Sometimes, you would look at him and not even say anything and just KNOW that before you did say anything, he had already read your mind."

Funny thing though...for all of his tricks, pranks, high jinks and shenanigans, Smarty Jones was a horse who clearly loved people, and craved their contact.

It wouldn't be long, before people felt exactly the same about him.

CHAPTER TWO

DOWN ON THE FARM

Much to the dismay of the racing purist, champion thoroughbreds aren't always born with a Kentucky Derby Trophy in their mouth. Not many offspring, even of the great Secretariat, were considered a "lock" to win a Triple Crown...and since there has been but one Triple Crown winner in the last almost three decades, one can easily conclude that "bloodstock" alone, does not a champion make.

By the same token, horses of what the same racing purist might refer to as, "questionable parentage," have on more than a few occasions, risen up and bitten the old blue-bloods in a place normally reserved for a tag bearing the name Saks Fifth Avenue.

Enter George Isaacs.

George is the General Manager of Bridlewood Farm, in Ocala, Florida. Every year, George, Trainer Milton Hendry and people just like them, take young thoroughbreds, known as "yearlings," wave a magic wand over their heads three times, recite "the magic words," and produce the next year's batch of winners.

If only it were that easy.

George has been in the business of breaking yearlings and turning them into real racehorses, for nearly thirty years. He has worked with many of the most successful racing champions of this era, including the current All-Time Leading Money Winner, "Cigar." George had also worked with Roy and Pat Chapman in the past, and was a dear friend of the Chapman's regular trainer, Bobby Camac.

Sometime in August, 2001, Bobby called George and talked about a "weanling" that he thought was to be "something special." George had known Bobby Camac for twenty-five years, and was more than a little bit excited about the prospect of working with the colt that he knew at this time, only as "Smarty."

Bobby was excited, too. After all, he was the one who had done the research. Smarty Jones was HIS ball of clay that he had begun molding and shaping more than four years ago when he initially convinced the Chapmans to purchase I'll Get Along. Bob had spent almost twice as much as Roy and Pat had initially authorized, in order to acquire the mare, but because he completely believed in what he was doing, Chappy did too and went along with the purchase. His creation took shape when he sold Roy and Pat on breeding her to Elusive Quality; and only six months into the horse's life, he was already telling his good friend George Isaacs that he would call him in December to arrange for Smarty to be shipped to Florida to begin his proper training.

Bobby Camac never called.

Instead, Roy Chapman called...to tell George that his dear friend, Bobby Camac, and his wife, Maryann, had been murdered by Maryann's son, Wade Russell. Roy and Pat were at their winter home in Florida when they were themselves informed that Bob and his wife were murdered. "He was a good man, and a good friend. It hurt Chappy, real bad." "Chappy had actually taken the call," Pat remembered. "It was Deb Given that notified us. Chappy had answered the phone, but then he just laid it down. When I asked him what was wrong, he couldn't even speak." "We were devastated," Pat Chapman lamented. "I still feel the shock, even today."

The Chapmans had already begun scaling down their racing operation several years earlier, for reasons relating to Chappy's health; and with Bob Camac now gone, they were fully prepared to sell the remainder of their barn and retire from racing for good. "Bob's death just seemed to take the life right out of Chappy," according to Pat. "He looked at me that very day and said, let's just get rid of everything."

Again, however, there was something about Smarty Jones that kept everything moving forward, even in the face of such a horrible tragedy.

Perhaps it was now simply the desire to follow through on Bob Camac's dream? There could be no more fitting tribute to a man who had earned the respect and enjoyed the friendship of virtually everyone he had encountered in the racing industry.

Perhaps it was Chappy holding out hope that Smarty Jones would be "the one" that he had been waiting for, for his entire racing career? Bob had not only convinced the Chapmans to acquire the mare and breed to a specific stud, he had also convinced them even in advance of the Smarty's arrival that he had a remarkable future ahead of him.

Perhaps the Chapmans just couldn't part with a horse which was named after Pat Chapman's mother, "The Original Smarty Jones"...especially since both "Smarties" were born on February 28th?

Whatever the reason...Smarty Jones remained in the Someday Farm Barn; and when George Isaacs was formally introduced to the steed on January 6, 2002, he was greeted by "a medium-sized colt, who was very correct...very athletic, and had a real way about him." The horse "walked with a real purpose," and had "no obvious confirmation faults." What he DID have, was a companion, in the form of the only other weanling that the Chapmans had elected to keep. George decided to keep the two horses together...and even though their real names were Smarty Jones and "Some Image"...everyone at Bridlewood Farm just called them, "The Chapman Boys."

The Chapman Boys were inseparable; and even though Some Image was exactly that...a HUGE horse, with the kind of incredible definition that might have given even the most confident companion a major inferiority complex...Smarty wasted no time in letting everyone know that "he was the boss of this field."

According to George, "Smarty showed up at Bridlewood acting almost as if he had been there before." "He wasn't tentative about anything. He wasn't cocky either, but he sure was confident." "He had a real shiny coat," Smarty's Trainer, Milton Hendry recalled. "You wouldn't pick him out of a

crowd for his size, but that coat caught your eye...
and his attitude certainly kept your attention."

"When you're raising horses," George said,
"they establish a pecking order real fast," and
Smarty had clearly established himself as the
leader. And, this was before anyone had seen him
run.

The first "speed work" that a yearling is called
upon to perform, is called "breezing." Breezing is
where a horse is asked to go at about ninety-five
percent speed, for first a sixteenth of a mile, then
later an eighth of a mile, and ultimately a quarter
mile. Twelve seconds is about what a trainer
expects from a good horse in his first eighth of a
mile breeze, twenty-four for a good quarter...maybe
twenty-six or twenty-seven, on the first try.

Smarty's first breeze was a full two seconds
faster than any other horse in the seventy-five
horse Class of 2002. Needless to say, George, Milton
Hendry, Smarty's Trainer at Bridlewood, and of
course the Chapmans, were now even more excited. Bobby Camac's ball of clay had already begun to
morph itself into a highly skilled, finely tuned work
of art, and no one was happier about this fact, than
George Isaacs.

Any "A-List" Trainer will tell you that most
"real runners" have a way about them, which sets
them apart from other horses. In Smarty's case, it
was that from his first day at Bridlewood Farm, "he
couldn't WAIT to get on the track." None of the
exercise riders who worked him, could hold him

back. According to Milton Hendry, "Smarty was this way before he even breezed for the first time." He was "an eager beaver... always up at his stall, with his head sticking out; not because he was nervous, but in his own way, just telling you...I WANT TO GO! This is like a dream for a trainer. By the time the horse gets to you, half of your work has already been done."

Milton Hendry has also worked with a number of great champions, but makes it very clear that Smarty Jones was the BEST two year old he had ever been around, because, "this horse told you from the moment he met you...I like my job."

"Thoroughbreds are all born and bred to race," Milton remarked, "but I never worked with a horse before, or since, that understood this game, at that age, like Smarty Jones. He was on a mission from the moment he got to the farm...and he wanted everyone to know it." Milton suggested that any number of horses come in with great pedigrees and "all the talent in the world," but they just don't "get it." "There's more to this game than just being able to run," he said. "The great ones ultimately figure that out and that's when they achieve that greatness. Smarty had it figured out before he ever got to the farm."

As '02 became '03...Smarty continued to put the vast majority of his contemporaries to shame. Smarty started out at the Head of the Class, and with every workout he added just a little more distance between himself and the rest of that same class.

Despite the fact that from a pure skill level Smarty was clearly ready to take on the world, Chappy didn't want to race him "too" early in his two year old season. By early April, however, there was a game plan in place to race Smarty at least once at Philadelphia Park, and if he was good enough, enter him in the Pennsylvania Futurity.

By late April, all bets were off... literally, as Smarty had "bucked his shin." The injury is fairly common, and not particularly serious, but it made sense to attempt to strengthen both shins at the same time, and this would delay the onset of Smarty's racing career.

While Chappy was once again disappointed... George was even more excited. "The slow ones never buck," he said.

Smarty certainly made a prophet out of George, too. In his first breeze after treatment and rehabilitation for bucking his shin, Smarty again "blew everything else on the track, away." He once again ran a full two seconds faster than every other horse on the farm, "and we were trying to hold him back."

The horse who showed up a year earlier with nothing more special about him, than a shiny coat and a killer personality, was now a mere van ride away from rewarding the fates for having gotten him this far.

Smarty Jones was ready...

...and on July 16, 2003, George called Chappy and told him so.

He also told his good friend, Roy Chapman, "this IS the one you have been waiting for."

He was the best two year old on the farm, and apparently George wasn't the only person to be particularly impressed. Milton Hendry was so confident of Smarty's future success that he did something he had never done before in connection with any of the thousands of horses that he has trained. "Before we shipped Smarty out, I had them put a brand new pair of shoes on him," Milton laughed. "I KNEW this horse was special, and that those shoes were gonna be worth something someday."

Word travels faster in the horse business than in a big city post office. Milton's Smarty shoes were apparently already worth quite a bit more than he thought. Before the doors on Smarty's van were closed, George was receiving inquiries about whether Smarty Jones was for sale.

Offers came in to buy the horse in the kinds of numbers that, "you just don't see in this business," for an untested commodity. Before one could be rejected, the next offer would be on his desk, in his mailbox, wisping out of a fax machine, or winging its' way to Ocala via the internet. Finally, he received an offer that George felt the Chapmans "couldn't refuse." When they did, George told them the potential buyer had agreed in advance to an even higher figure.

Pat Chapman took the lead this time, and made it clear, that they were "going to ride this horse as far as he would take them." "There might have been a time when Chappy at least wanted to talk about it, I mean, after all, no one we talked to could believe the kind of money that was being offered. In all honesty though, there was no amount of money that was going to change our life, or the way we lived it," Pat went on. "We owed it to Bob, and to Smarty, and to my mother, and to ourselves, to share this horse, and this experience with the world."

Once George had officially rejected (on the Chapmans' behalf) the last of the flood of offers to buy Smarty Jones, he sat down with the them to begin formally plotting out the course of Smarty's racing career. George was convinced that Smarty was going to take the racing world by storm. He thought that Roy and Pat needed to take advantage of every opportunity as well as every angle. Smarty was "definitely a New York-style horse," George told his friends...industry code which meant that the horse had a lot of ability, and needed to be housed at a good track, with a good trainer.

Enter John Servis.

CHAPTER THREE

AT YOUR SERVIS

Famed author, George Plimpton once told a story about a final examination that he had taken while attending Oxford University. The final exam consisted of one question; which asked the students to identify a specific individual, and to remark upon his contribution to society. Plimpton recalled that from the reaction of he and his fellow students, it was clear that not so much as a single one of his colleagues had any idea who this person was...or what he might have done to warrant inclusion on the exam.

As late as July 16, 2003, the name on George Plimpton's Oxford final examination might just as easily have been John Servis. A few days later... John Servis was the new Trainer, of Smarty Jones.

In all fairness, John WAS something of a known quantity in racing. He was successful enough to keep a barn full of forty-five horses under his charge, and had more than earned his chops in the racing business. But, up to the time that Smarty Jones trotted off of the same van as Some Image...if you asked John if he thought he would be nine months away from standing in the Winner's Circle at Churchill Downs...chances are, even HE would honestly tell you, "NO WAY!"

Then again, what at ALL, about the life and times of Smarty Jones, to this point or beyond, would be "normal," "routine," or "the way things are supposed to happen?"

John Servis got his first job training horses in 1981. Like his Uncle Jack, John had been a jockey's agent prior to that time...and it was through his uncle, that he met and ultimately became close friends with Mark Reid. Mark was an established trainer, who knew that John wanted to become a trainer someday, as well. In late 1981, Mark hired John as his Assistant Trainer; and after three years, was instrumental in John going out on his own for the first time.

The friendship didn't end when John left Mark's barn. In fact, the two became even closer... not just as individuals, but as a family, also. The horses which Mark had given to John in order to fill his first barn, kept them close in a business context. Naming John, Godfather to the Reids' youngest son, welded a strong family tie between the two men that would last a lifetime.

Mark Reid had also trained horses at one time, for Roy and Pat Chapman; before Bobby Camac.

When it was time to ship Smarty from Florida, and there was no barn, or trainer to ship him to... Chappy first asked George Isaacs for a recommendation...and later got in touch with his former trainer, Mark Reid. Mark was no longer training thoroughbreds. He was now a fulltime bloodstock agent, living in Maryland.

George had already told Chappy that he needed a trainer who was not only "good," but was also not afraid to travel. Mark Reid suggested that the Chapmans might be equally comfortable with his former assistant, John Servis, OR a Maryland-based trainer named Tony Dutrow.

Shortly after making his recommendation to the Chapmans, Mark Reid contacted John Servis directly. Mark told his friend that the Chapmans were looking for a trainer, for what might be a very special horse. Reid also told Servis that he had recommended him to the Chapmans, and that "they might be calling you."

Keep in mind that John Servis was, at the time, a working professional trainer...who had a full barn. He was not out soliciting new clients. Keep in mind, that EVERY owner...tells EVERY trainer, or prospective trainer...that EVERY horse is "special," "gifted," or on its' way to the Derby. So, even when John was told by his friend, former boss, and equine mentor, that "the Chapmans think they have some-thing really special," John's FIRST reaction was to think, "yeah...right" and leave it at that. If they called, they called...if not, John still had plenty of work to do with his other horses.

Roy Chapman did call; the very next day as a matter of fact. The Chapmans had met John Servis, some years earlier, at the home of Mark Reid; during a graduation party for Mark's oldest son. They really didn't remember him, however...nor he them. They knew that John was having some degree of success as a trainer based out of Philadelphia Park; and the Chapmans themselves were well-known to the entire Philadelphia Park family of horsemen.

The Chapmans DID know Tony Dutrow; not personally, but by a reputation which was by all accounts, more substantial at that time, than that of John Servis. In fact, had it not been that John was based closer to their home; affording Roy and Pat a greater opportunity to maintain personal contact with Smarty Jones; even Mark Reid thought that the Chapmans would probably have given the two horses over to him.

"There were a lot of people that were sur-prised that we picked John," Roy Chapman related. "Dutrow was much better known, nationwide... much better." "However," his wife added, "John was a Philadelphia Boy...just like Smarty Jones."

Loyalty is very important to Pat Chapman. It is one of the benchmarks of her existence. They had worked horses out of other tracks in the past, but to them, Philadelphia Park was home. They were Philly people and Philly Park people, as well. If they could bring a great horse to Philadelphia Park and allow the racetrack itself to share in and perhaps benefit from the resulting notoriety, they would do exactly that, because that is the kind of people that they are. You stick by them and they will be there for you. If John hadn't been based out of Philadelphia Park, chances are...Smarty Jones still would have been.

During their first phone call, Chappy told John that he had two horses; Smarty Jones, and Some Image. Chappy mentioned that the horses were already on their way to Pennsylvania, from Bridlewood Farm, in Florida; and that he had hoped to house them at Philadelphia Park, which was closest to the Chapmans home, in New Hope, Pennsylvania. Roy Chapman was every bit as excited about these horses...particularly Smarty Jones; as Mark Reid had earlier suggested. John remained less than convinced, for the moment, that there was anything really "special" about either of The Chapman Boys, but agreed to take the horses into his barn. George Isaacs later contacted John, offering words of encouragement, and telling him exactly how excited HE was about Smarty, also.

Sometimes, in every truly amazing story, you really do have to pause more than once, and simply play "the WHAT IF game." This is one such time.

WHAT IF...the Chapmans had never switched trainers, from Mark Reid, to Bob Camac, in the first place?

WHAT IF...I'll get Along was left to foal in Kentucky?

WHAT IF...Bob Camac was still alive?

WHAT IF...the Chapmans had given Smarty to Tony Dutrow?

WHAT IF...John was TOO busy to take on ANY new horses?

The point here is simply that throughout the Smarty Jones saga, you come to a rather rapid realization that there wasn't "one thing," or even a series of things which HAD to "go right," in order for this horse and the people around him, to touch so many, in the ways that they did. There were events occurring, literally ANY ONE OF WHICH could have changed EVERYTHING; making the only appropriate answer then, to every "WHAT IF" question; "So what?"

The Chapmans DID offer the horses to John Servis, and he DID accept them.

A short time later, The Chapman Boys arrived on the same van, from Florida; and when they trotted off that van...the crew at the John Servis stable was SURE, for the first time, that they DID have a winner on their hands.

This horse was HUGE...and BEAUTIFUL...and POWERFUL...and turned EVERY head, at every one of the surrounding barns. John's first reaction, "...this was the most imposing physical specimen I have ever seen."

Unfortunately, John and the crew would find

out a moment later, that THIS horse's name was "Some Image."

When "the OTHER horse," exited the van a few moments later, John's Assistant, Maureen Donnelly branded him, "the shrimp"...Bill Foster, John's 6'5" Barn manager literally TOWERED over him; and John thought, "...well...he'll probably make a good sprinter."

The momentary elation which had been enjoyed by all in attendance was rather rapidly replaced by John thinking, "WHAT have I gotten myself into?" "Chappy thinks this horse is going to be a STAR."

John was so distressed at his initial eyeballing of the horse that he was moved to immediately put in a call to George Isaacs to "cool his jets a little bit." John told George, "You've got Chappy so pumped up...and this horse hasn't even been to the track yet. You've got him thinking he's going to the Derby already. You gotta give me a break." George remembers almost openly laughing when John's call came in. "Call me after he gets to the track," George told the young trainer. "If you're still concerned, then we can talk."

Fortunately for all concerned, Smarty and Some Image actually DID make it to the racetrack, a few days later, for their first work out. The whole barn, and many people from other Philly Park Barns were curious.

The track itself, while recognized as having perhaps one of the best surfaces in all of racing, will never be confused with the likes of Churchill Downs, Sartoga, or any of the other "Grand Old" thoroughbred racing venues. One New York Newspaper even once referred to the facility as a third-rate track, in a second rate town, and followed that with even less flattering references to the people who work at or even frequent the facility. Perhaps this is why, when a locally respected trainer like John Servis had let a few people know that The Chapmans were putting two horses in his barn, EVERYBODY from the backside showed up to see them workout. They all wanted to see what the "new meat" had to show for themselves.

As The Chapman Boys made their way to the track that morning, John watched, from aboard his trusted and long time friend, "Butterscotch," while Maureen, Bill and the others stood at the rail.

Pete Van Trump, John's slightly over-sized exercise rider was aboard Smarty Jones, who was still being referred to, for the moment, as either, **"the OTHER horse,"** or by friends of Roy and Pat Chapman as **"And, By The Way"**...a name they had given him during a visit to Bridlewood Farm; where they TOO were consumed with the beauty of Some Image.

A mere thirty seconds later, however, Smarty Jones would NEVER AGAIN be referred to as anything other than, "A Champion."

You only get one opportunity on life to make a good first impression. This was nothing new to Smarty Jones, however, he had been making simply remarkable first impressions throughout the course of his entire young life. He would treat this group of new friends, this day, to a similar introduction.

So...as Smarty Jones BLISTERED the track, with 170 pounds of Pete Van Trump, "HOLDING ON FOR DEAR LIFE"...and literally every person at the park both shocked and in awe...the backside whisperers all wanted to know, "WHO IS THAT...WHO IS THAT?" John and Butterscotch did their best to simply catch up to their new best friend, while Maureen openly screamed, "FINALLY...someone was RIGHT in their assessment of a horse!"

Pete Van Trump grew up in Missouri, and had been riding horses almost before he could even walk. He was now, "so excited" he "couldn't even speak." "He left that other horse (this time referring to Some Image) like he was standing still. None of us expected ANYTHING like that. John was so far behind me, I couldn't even SEE him. It took him a good thirty seconds, just to get up to where I was finally able to STOP my horse."

The John Servis Stable was ECSTATIC! In one workout, they knew EXACTLY what they had.

They had SMARTY JONES!

It was now John Servis, who needed to take a deep breath, and realize that the fates had just knocked at HIS door, and invited themselves in for a cup of coffee, in order to discuss HIS future... which, strangely enough did NOT include a second phone call to George Isaacs.

When I asked John why he never called George back, he smiled...then laughed, and finally said, "What was I going to say? You were right, I'm an idiot? I wasn't going to do that...plus, we still had a LONG way to go."

George was definitely right, but trust me, John is no idiot. He will be a star in the racing business for decades to come. But, if this experience did anything for John Servis, it reminded him that you really can't judge a book by its' cover. In fact, John so wanted to make up for his initial visual slighting of Smarty that shortly after this particular workout, he began introducing Smarty to people as "my big horse." John's wife Sherry chuckled when he told me this, recalling her own introduction to Smarty Jones. "That's what he called him the first day I ever saw Smarty, too. I remember thinking, he doesn't look all THAT big. The other one, now...he was just plain huge."

Oh...and speaking of judging a book by its' cover ...what ever became of Some Image?

Interestingly enough, both John Servis and Roy Chapman would at different times, use the exact same words to describe the big horse's racing future.

"He couldn't beat ME around the track!"

Chappy clearly still has a soft spot in his heart for "the BIG horse," however. "They should DEFINITELY put that horse on a calendar or something. He is a magnificent animal...he just can't run."

CHAPTER FOUR

<u>HELLO MODO</u>

As an athlete, or in life generally, of course everyone wants to "win the big one." It isn't insomnia which has Olympic hopefuls practicing while the rest of the world sleeps. People who buy Powerball Lottery tickets, don't usually kneel in church and pray to have, oh...say "three" of the six winning numbers.

I found it funny to learn that more people win gold medals in the Olympics which occur each four years, than will win Powerball Lottery jackpots, in the same four year period.

Just think...how much more disappointed you would feel though, if you MADE it to the Olympics, and another competitor's friend hit you in the knee with a pipe before you could perform? Or, even worse...you had all SIX numbers in the Powerball Lottery...and left the ticket in your pants pocket when you washed your pants.

By July 2003, and for his entire existence on this planet; Smarty Jones had done everything in his power to tell everyone who had come in contact with him, that he was on his way to the big game. When HE wasn't broadcasting that fact by way of his own limited track exploits, the racing Gods were playing Puppet Master in virtually all parts of the world, just to make sure there was no mistaking that this horse had an as of yet unfulfilled mission.

Smarty was rapidly becoming known by those who would further guide him, as someone who should have a big "S" on his chest, regardless of the first letter of his real name. He had snatched life from the jaws of death himself, witnessed the death of the man who was responsible for giving him life; and had not only passed every test presented to him in the intervening two years, but had done so with flying colors...and while creating an expectation in others, that there was absolutely NOTHING which he could not do.

All that remained, was the little matter of a Starting Gate.

In this instance, however, it was Smarty's greatest asset, that would prove also, to be his greatest liability. Smarty's dominant pedigree was that of a sprinter. What kept him on his toes all the time, and wanting to "GO" all the time; and more excited about being on the track than other horses, was that part of a sprinter which simply can't sit still. Clearly, Smarty was a horse that, if he COULD talk, would be mumbling constantly; "Gotta GO...c'mon, let me outta here... gotta RUN!"

Most sprinters are never comfortable in the starting gate. After all, they want to RUN. At Bridlewood Farm, Smarty was never comfortable in the starting gate, either. Milton Hendry said, "He was never afraid of the gate, but he was always antsy inside. He would walk right in, but you just knew that he could blow up in there, at any time."

And blow up...he did.

Less than three weeks into his residence at the John Servis Stable, the racing career, and the life of Smarty Jones both hung in the balance.

Smarty was in a practice starting gate, with Pete Van Trump in the saddle, and Maureen Donnelly preparing to open the gate. He had walked in, as he had so many times in Florida; no problem. Maureen started to come in, but before she could get there, Smarty reared, and at the same time lunged, as if almost to attempt to hurdle himself out of the gate, which by his own standard, just wasn't opening fast enough.

The horse hit his head on an iron bar atop the gate, and to the extent possible, went down in a heap, inside the gate, with Pete still aboard.

He began to thrash, uncontrollably, for approximately a minute. When one of the training assistants was able to revive Smarty, he finally managed to get back up on his feet and out of the gate.

In a matter of those same sixty seconds, Smarty's face was covered with blood. At first, Pete thought he had simply bloodied his nose. This happens quite often to two year olds, and as in the case of humans, the situation sometimes looks far worse than it really is.

Pete knew he needed to get the horse back to the barn and get him cleaned up...so, still in the saddle, the two headed for the gap and down the horse path.

At some point along the way, that sixth or even seventh sense that every good horseman possesses, made Pete know that he needed to get off of the horse and take a closer look, even before they reached the barn. In an instant, he knew, "this was serious." "He was all busted up," Pete remembers.

"His eye and whole head were already starting to swell up, and there was blood coming out of everywhere."

Even before Smarty reached his stall, an emergency call went out over the backside public address system for Dr. Dan Hanf, to come to Barn 11, immediately. On his arrival, Dr. Hanf (on his very first day covering for John's regular veterinarian, Dr. Clyman) found the horse in significant distress. He had a huge gash on the top of his head, and was "profusely gushing blood out of both nostrils, and his mouth, as well." The external head wound was washed out repeatedly, but there was nothing that was being done that could stop the bleeding. "We sedated him to reduce his blood pressure and tried to comfort him as best as we could."

"He bled for over an hour," according to Dr. Hanf. "But once we got it stopped, he seemed alert, responsive, and acting as though he was going to be alright." Smarty was checked several times throughout the remainder of the day, and while he looked, "uglier and uglier," at least to this veterinarian, "he was otherwise acting pretty normal." Antibiotics and anti-inflammatories were administered to guard against infection and reduce swelling in the area around the wound, and a decision was made to have Dr. Hanf revisit the animal at 6 AM, to determine a further course of treatment.

Dr. Hanf last checked Smarty's head at about 4 PM, and left the barn confident that he was at least stable and that his head, "was about as big as it could possibly get."

When he did return that following morning, Dr. Hanf could simply not believe what he found.

By 6 AM, Smarty's head had swollen to three times its' normal size, and was not only filling with fluid, but also air...indicating that his sinus cavities were cracked, and that air was forcing its' way into other areas of his skin.

Pete remarked that the horse looked "like someone had beaten it in the head with a sledge hammer."

Bill Foster, John's Barn Manager and Smarty's best friend, was certain that the horse was not going to survive the ordeal. The flesh around his eye had completely engulfed the eye and it could no longer be seen. John simply remembers, "It was absolutely the grossest thing you ever saw. There were at least three or four inches of tissue which had pushed out from where the eye USED to be. It scared the hell out of me."

Without hesitation, Dr. Hanf directed that an immediate call be placed to the New Jersey Equine Center; where Dr. Patricia Hogan was notified that she would soon be receiving an emergency case that was "a real mess." Dr. Hanf believed that Smarty's left eye had completely ruptured.

Dr. Hanf also believed, for the first time, that the horse's life was in danger.

Dr. Hogan was in surgery at the time the call came in, but was advised that the emergency case was being brought in to, at the very least, have his left eye removed.

Not knowing exactly what to expect when the horse arrived, Dr. Hogan anticipated the worst of all possible scenarios.

Imagine her surprise, when the doors to Smarty's van opened up and he came trotting off of the van, "dragging the guy on his lead," as if to say, "I guess you're all wondering why I called you here, today?"

Dr. Hogan also noted that the horse's head "had in fact, swollen to more than three times his normal size" and that there was "bleeding from the left nostril, with his eye swollen completely shut," but that his ears were up, and he appeared "spunky."

According to Dr. Hogan, Smarty was every bit the "mess" that had been suggested by Dr. Hanf.

Dr. Hogan's first impression of Smarty Jones; "Where do we start? He looked so bad, I thought... I've seen all of these injuries before, just never at the same time."

A more detailed examination conducted by Dr. Hogan, revealed that Smarty's eye had not actually ruptured, and would not have to be removed. He did however, have multiple fractures of the skull, including the frontal sinus, forehead, nasal bone and eye socket. His left eye was finally located, but was under a full three inches of tissue. He was given anti-inflammatory drugs injected directly into the eye socket, antibiotics, and placed in thick, padded bandaging, to the point where the only part of his head which was then visible, was his right eye, and the very tips of his ears.

Dr. Hogan thought that he looked "like a burn victim." The rest of the staff at the clinic just started calling him "Quasimodo." Of course this was after it had been determined that Smarty had made it out of the woods, so to speak. "I just couldn't understand or believe, that a horse who was in such terrible, horrible shape was able to act almost as if this was just another day in his life," an almost amazed Patti Hogan remarked. "No other horse could have dealt with all of those injuries the way Smarty did. It was unbelievable."

With the remainder of his future still very much in doubt, Smarty still acted as though he had everything very much under control. The humans, on the other hand, were in some sense, a bigger "mess" than he was.

For John Servis; this was the first horse that he had trained for the Chapmans and, "the last thing I wanted to have to do, was call Chappy, and tell him that this horse that he had heard all of these great things about for the last six months, was in trouble."

As it was, John will never forget the first

phone call he made to Chappy regarding the incident. Neither will Roy Chapman. "As soon as John called me and said, We had a little problem with one of the horses...right away I said, It's Smarty, isn't it?" "When John said yes...I thought I was going to be sick."

In fact, the entire training staff at the John Servis Stable was made sick by the incident. On the day of the accident, they all hoped that a trip to the hospital would not be necessary...and when Smarty was still bleeding, but dove his swelled head into the food tray as it was making its' way past his stall...they thought he was going to be just fine.

On the day after the accident, "this place was like a morgue," one of the grooms remarked. "After they took Smarty away, none of us expected to see him again." Still worried about having to tell Chappy it was worse than he first thought, John was too nervous to even answer the phone on any of the nineteen occasions when Dr. Hogan attempted to call him, that day. "I was probably ducking her," John admitted. "When Smarty left here, I thought the worst. Whatever she would be calling me about, I knew it wasn't going to be good."

Ultimately he was fine, but here too, Smarty earned an even greater respect from every human who had made his acquaintance throughout the ordeal.

Maureen Donnelly, who has been in the racing business for over twenty-five years, said, "Two year olds have accidents like this all the time. Some of them make it, and some don't. The only thing that got Smarty Jones through this accident...was Smarty Jones."

Dr. Hogan agreed. She called Smarty, "a good patient, who trusted people." "He was always interested in his treatment, and looking at us, as if to say, what are you guys going to do to me, next?"

Even as "Quasimodo," Smarty let everyone know how different he was. He never missed a meal; not only on the day of his accident, but for every one of the fourteen days he was in the hospital, as well. And, when placed in the stall right by the entrance door to the clinic, he STILL stuck his supersized, burn victim, Quasimodo head, right in the face of everyone who came in or out; just to let them know that Smarty Jones was in the house. This prompted some at the clinic to re-nickname Smarty, "The Party Guy."

The question remained, however, would Smarty Jones ever actually race? Would he ever be able to walk into a starting gate again, without being hampered by the memory of his accident?

For the six weeks that he spent recuperating and rehabilitating at Cedar Lane Farm prior to returning to the The John Servis Stable, no one could answer either of these questions. "I had no idea how he would react when he got back to the barn," John Servis said. "You just can't expect that any horse would be able to put something like what happened to Smarty, out of their mind, totally."

On his first day back in the barn however,

Smarty Jones announced to the world once again, that he was not just "any horse."

Bill Foster, John's Barn Manager remarked, "He wasn't back in that barn for five minutes, before you knew he was thinking, C'mon...what are you guys waiting for? We got work to do!" "There's not another horse in the world that coulda come back from that," Bill said...and then he just smiled. The rest of the staff was even more amazed and impressed by the animal than ever.

Those who had last seen him beaten, bloodied and literally staring death directly in the face, openly wept and cheered as Smarty headed to the track on the morning of his first post-accident workout.

When recalling Smarty's return to the race-track Dr. Hogan was beaming, bordering on glowing. Through one of the biggest smiles I have ever seen came the words, "Smarty's head could have swelled to TEN times its' normal size...and it still wouldn't have been as big as his heart. He is one VERY special animal."

As John thought back to that moment, where Smarty was making his way to the track again for the first time after the accident, he recalled, "I was right about here, just like I am now...up on the pony and watching him. I remember thinking, I can't believe that he can come back out here and just pick up where he left off. If you didn't KNOW he had this accident, you would never guess it from the way he charged back onto the track. And then I thought...hey he's a Philly horse. He's one tough little son of a gun."

Chapter Five

LET THE GAMES BEGIN

From cradle to grave, horseracing is a never ending series of one "game" after another; one giant chess board with an entire row of new "knights" every year, the rest pawns, and no real king or queen. Individuals of modest means, in many instances, compete on something of a level plane with the world's oldest money, as well as dot-com, Gen X billionaires and Middle Eastern guardians of the world's fossil fuel supply.

In the Spring and Summer of 2003, a rag-tag group of high school buddies from Long Island, took a particularly unlikely prospect named "Funny Cide" to within two minutes of winning thorough-bred racing's coveted Triple Crown. Two months later, a successful automobile dealer, his wife and an upstart young horse trainer would meet in sub-urban Philadelphia in an effort to construct a plan to eliminate those two minutes, and make racing history in their own right.

Smarty Jones was regaining his strength and preparing for his first race. Still however, for the horse Chappy just knew was "destined for great-ness," a number of significant questions remained ...all of which amounted to just another in the laun-dry list of games, yet to be played out.

In no particular order, all of the following would soon require an answer.

WHO would be Smarty's Rider?

WHAT was Smarty really capable of; given his injuries?

WHEN would Smarty's ultimate journey begin?

WHERE should Smarty be introduced to the world?

WHY did John, Pat and Roy Chapman STILL "believe" that an unknown trainer, from a perceived second-rate racetrack, could take a $10,000 horse and make a star out of him?

HOW would they ever get Smarty Jones back into a starting gate?

The "WHAT" portion of the equation would for

the most part be left up Smarty Jones; and given what he had already been through to this point in his short life, "Team Smarty" knew that once they handed the ball off to the animal, he would be a game competitor every step of the way.

There was a decided difference of opinion early on, however, with regard to "WHERE" Smarty's racing career should commence. Before the horse had even been transported from Florida, to Philadelphia Park, George Isaacs had been lobbying the Chapmans to have the horse "break his maiden" in New York. George still believed that Smarty was a tremendous prospect. He also knew that Roy and Pat had turned down "psychotic" money from people who wanted to own this horse. Winning his first race, or breaking his maiden, in New York, would dramatically increase his value, immediately. "The price would have gone sky high," George said. Smarty would receive more immediate exposure to the racing elite, as well as derive substantially more media attention. It didn't hurt that Chappy kinda has a thing for the ambience of the grand old racetrack which is, Saratoga, either.

John Servis, was of a completely different mindset. What with not one, but ALL of the difficulties that had been faced by this horse, just to get to the point where finally getting onto the racetrack again was possible; John wanted Smarty's first race to be "a pleasant experience."

Going to New York would require travel, and added attention to a horse that, "we still didn't really know anything about." "Keep it simple," John told the Chapmans. "Let him go out the first time at Philadelphia Park." John thought the pace would be "easier," the experience "quieter," there would be no travel, and that Smarty would run against slightly lesser competition than he might encounter had the move been made to take the show on the road, so soon.

It was also John's call when it came to the "WHO" portion of the previous inquiry. With the Chapman's approval, John gave Smarty's initial mount to Stewart Elliott. Ironically, as you will see later in this work, "WHO"...Stew, would become "Stew WHO," by the time Smarty made it to the Kentucky Derby. But, let's not get ahead of ourselves.

John selected Stewart Elliott, because he knew him. He had used him as a jockey before, in connection with many of John's other horses, and thought that he was a gifted rider. "He coulda been anywhere," John said. "He's a very good rider, that shouldn't be here (at Philly Park)."

Stewart's "demons" have been more than adequately addressed throughout much of the mass media coverage of the Smarty Jones Story. John was fully aware of the situation at the time he considered Stew for Smarty's first race. In fact, several years earlier, when John took a Filly named "Jostle" to the 2000 Coaching Club American Oaks at Belmont Park and the Alabama Stakes at Saratoga, he had taken Stewart off of the horse, because of those very same demons. Since that time however, he had watched Stewart empower himself, and take control over his life, and felt more than comfortable that given the opportunity, Stewart Elliott would do as good of a job guiding Smarty Jones, as anyone.

The Chapman's knew Stewart Elliott, both by name, and by his association with Philadelphia Park. They weren't moved either way, positively or negatively, at John's choice, but they DID, trust John Servis. "You hire a trainer," Chappy chimed in, "you let him train. If you want to make all of the decisions yourself, don't hire a trainer." In the same fashion in which Chappy had left all of the breeding decisions up to Bobby Camac, he had confidently placed the future of this great racehorse in the hands of John Servis...and there would be no turning back.

Stewart Elliott, would escort Smarty Jones into and hopefully out of his first REAL Starting Gate, at Philadelphia Park...but when?

It was early-September 2003, and Smarty Jones was still "at the farm" recuperating from his accident. It would be weeks until he even returned to the barn, and at least an additional day, until he would find himself face to face with the very same practice starting gate, which put him out of action in the first place.

As was stated earlier however, when it would come to matters that were within the exclusive control of Smarty Jones, there seemed relatively little with which to be concerned. John, like essentially everyone who is fortunate enough to get to know this animal, stopped seeing Smarty AS "an animal" very early on in the relationship. "He doesn't DO, what other horses do...or ACT like other horses act," he told me.

From personal experience; you can look at Smarty Jones, and the significance is not that you know WHAT he is thinking...but that you know THAT he is thinking. John told me, "this horse just doesn't spook." "Horses spook all the time, but this one...he could be walking down the path and have the roof blow off of a barn and land in front of him, and he would stop, look at it, and say...I, think I'll take a turn and go around that thing." John also told me about strangers coming into the barn. Every other horse in the forty-five stall barn would become routinely agitated, and let everyone know it, pretty fast. Smarty...he would eyeball the new-comer from top to bottom as if to say, "Hey...Smarty Jones, here...damn glad to meet you." When I entered Philadelphia Park's now famous Barn 11, the first time, I can tell you that I was greeted by each of its' residents in exactly this fashion.

The question remained however, how WOULD Smarty react, the first time he was asked to go back into the gate.

Bill Foster was emphatic when he said that Smarty was in the barn for only five minutes after returning from the farm, before he wanted to get out and head for the track. But, on that day, September 21, 2003, when Smarty made his way to the track for the first time since the accident... John said, "When Smarty got to the gate, I saw fear in his eyes, for the first and only time." "He wanted no parts of it." According to Pete Van Trump, "he didn't back up. He didn't refuse...but, he gave it a good look for about maybe thirty seconds" before he thought, "I guess I gotta do this."

And do it, he did.

The gate opened, and Smarty did exactly what he was born to do...run. Like the thrown rider who is told he must "get back up on the horse" right away...this "horse" got back into the gate, and then right out of it with no problem; answering any questions anyone might have had about his personal commitment to excellence.

Smarty had done his part. The rest was up to John and now Stewart, and the remainder of Team Smarty.

John wasted no time going right back to work. As trainers go, John Servis is something of a charts and graphs kinda guy, when it comes to plotting out where a horse should run, when he should run, and in what specific races he should be entered. He is methodic bordering on mad when it comes to detail, and attention to detail in the management of a horse's racing career...but ever mindful of the fact that madness without method, is the benchmark of failure. He doesn't simply enter eight horses in an eight horse race in an attempt to boost his own numbers. He is more concerned about his owners and their horses being successful than he is seeing his own name at the top of the "winningest this or that list."

In Smarty's case, the horse's training continued while John looked over the next few months worth of racing cards. He would find the right place and right time to bring Smarty out, and he would do it the old-fashioned way. He would look his horse in the eye and see clear through to his soul and know that the time was right. He would rely on his assistants and his rider, as well as his instincts make the decision to introduce Smarty Jones to the world.

With everything right in Smarty's world, John ultimately decided to green light the animal on a brisk November afternoon...November 9, 2003, to be exact.

In a field of unknowns, this day, Smarty Jones was just another name on the program. Before the bell, any one or every one of the horses in that field could have been on their way to the Derby. But, when the wire photo was taken, and it would be seven-and-a-half lengths before another horse would enter the picture, the first piece of the Smarty Puzzle, had been securely placed on the table.

"It was a great ride," John said. "I was really impressed. Stew didn't have to whip him, not once. He did everything that was asked of him, and then some." Little did anyone in the park know, on that cool autumn afternoon, in what will never be described as the racing capital of the universe, that they had just witnessed a preview of the most exciting story to consume the thoroughbred landscape, and all of sports, in perhaps their collective lifetime.

Dr. Hogan remembers calling John shortly after Smarty's first win and telling him, "We did it." While everyone associated with Team Smarty was publicly hoping that the horse could still realize their own dream; Dr. Hogan and John Servis had more than a few times since the accident, agreed that a more realistic goal was simply to get this racehorse INTO a race. Privately, both doubted that he would ever win...anything. "Just seeing him race, was a victory," Dr. Hogan said. "Winning, was a bonus."

No longer untested; his accident no longer more than a blip on a medical chart, Smarty Jones was prepared to dive into a much bigger sandbox...albeit still at Philadelphia Park. On only two weeks rest, John Servis announced his intentions to the racing community, by entering his protégé in the 2003 Pennsylvania Nursery Stakes.

The race was slightly longer. The racing competition was somewhat stiffer. Smarty didn't make it any easier on himself either, when he stumbled out of the gate, and nearly went down on the track. Of course, once he got up, he didn't make it easy on the rest of the field; going on to win the race by fifteen lengths.

Most noteworthy of the contest, was not even

that Smarty had gone from a near fall to such a dramatic margin of victory; but moreso that once AGAIN, Stewart Elliott had not once taken the whip to his charge.

In an abbreviated two year old season, Smarty Jones was now two starts; two wins. He had a "Beyer Speed Rating" which was one of the highest in history, for any two year old. He also had owners who were now receiving offers to buy him, from as far away as California, to the west; England and Ireland, to the east. So, while Pat and Chappy fended off contact "from this one bloodstock agent in Miami who just kept calling, and calling...and CALLING," John Servis sent out for another case of "midnight oil" in an effort to aid him in his quest to identify the next step on the "Road to Success."

John still had more than a little cause for concern, however. Smarty was "way behind" where he should have been, from both a training and racing perspective and John knew it. Most two year olds begin their racing season long before November 9th; especially if anyone in the racing business thinks the horse has any real promise. "Hell," John said, "Smarty was a three year old and he hadn't even been around two turns yet."

Smarty's accident may have kept him a bit more "fresh" than two year olds who kick it off much earlier in the year, but in John's mind also cost him any opportunity at winning the title of Two Year Old Champion. It also made those closest to the horse wonder if there was any way they could ever possibly get him ready to make a legitimate run at the Derby.

"When Smarty Jones ran his first two races, he broke out of the gate and ran, with Stewart just hanging on for dear life," John recalled. "All he knew was when that gate opened, he was supposed to go, and to go as far as he could go, as fast as he could go. That's all he knew."

When Smarty won the Nursery Stakes with an even higher Beyer Speed Rating that was almost literally off the charts, most of the local media and many racing fans were saying, "WOW! What a horse!" All John Servis could say was, "I gotta slow this horse down. He doesn't realize he can't run the first part of every race the way he's running now."

John knew that if he could teach Smarty to "bottle his speed" and use it at the end of a race, he would in fact have a VERY special horse.

CHAPTER SIX

ALL ROADS LEAD TO...

ARKANSAS?

Within days following Smarty's victory in the Nursery Stakes, John Servis told Roy Chapman, "If we win the Count Fleet, we're going to Arkansas." Chappy's response was short, not so sweet, and very to the point. "Arkansas?"

John repeated his intentions. Chappy expanded upon his reply. "We live in FLORIDA, John. Why not send him to FLORIDA?" John didn't back down. He reminded Chappy that only a few months ago, his instructions were, "...get us to the Derby," and that is exactly what he intended to do.

But, Arkansas? "I had no more ambition to go to Arkansas, than the Man in the Moon," Chappy laughed. "We had confidence in John though, and when he laid out the plan...we bought into it. All we had to do now was get through the Count Fleet."

The Count Fleet Stakes, an event named after one of Smarty's direct ancestors, would run in January 2004, at Aqueduct Raceway in New York. The race would take Smarty Jones on his first ever trip around two turns, and give John Servis the degree of confidence he felt he needed to make the Run for the Roses...or not.

When the entries for the Count Fleet were complete, there was little speed in the race. John knew Smarty would break quickly and probably want to get to the front early. In pre-race instructions, John repeatedly admonished Stewart Elliott to get the horse to relax. Since his victory in the Nursery Stakes, getting this horse to "relax" had been the sole and exclusive focus of Smarty's training. Stewart didn't have to worry about settling, or relaxing Smarty in his first two races. The distances were shorter, and in both races, Smarty stumbled out of the gate, caught the field and then blew right by them on his way to victory. As it turned out when the gates opened at Aqueduct, Smarty stumbled again...the third time, in three races. John's pre-race instructions were immediately tossed into the cylindrical file. John didn't have to worry about Smarty rushing to the front. Stewart didn't have to worry about relaxing the horse. Stew just hung on, one more time...and a half mile later, Smarty caught up to the leaders, passed them, and went on to win the Count Fleet Stakes by five lengths.

The good news...Team Smarty was 3-0 and on its' way to Arkansas.

The bad news...John still had no idea if his horse was capable of settling.

The decision to let Smarty "grow up" in Arkansas was still a hard one for Chappy to accept, but it was a very easy one for John to make. Traditionally, at the start of each new racing year, the perceived best three year olds in the world end up in Florida. They come to Florida to impress the racing experts and elitists, in search of their approval, as well as the designation as "frontrunner" on the way to Kentucky. They also beat each other up, go nose to nose until legs, tendons, ligaments and other body parts stop functioning properly, and run themselves right out of any Derby opportunity.

By John's own admission, Smarty's first three victories had not only shown that he had trouble getting out of the gate without nearly stumbling; they had also demonstrated that this horse was, "speed crazy." "If we took him to Florida before we taught him to bottle his speed, and against that kind of competition, he would never learn to relax...and he could have gotten hurt." Arkansas seemed by far the easier way to go to accomplish what Smarty would HAVE to accomplish, if the rest of Team Smarty would ever accomplish what they all HOPED to accomplish.

The Oaklawn Jockey Club in Hot Springs, Arkansas, had three great Pre-Kentucky Derby preparatory races. John loved everything about the races, especially how they might work to the distinct advantage of Smarty Jones. John liked the timing of the races, and also the way in which their distances stretched out.

The first of the Arkansas Trilogy, The Southwest Stakes, would test Smarty at a mile. The Rebel Stakes would ask him to handle a mile and a sixteenth. The last in the series, The Arkansas Derby, would up the ante to a mile and an eighth, and with any luck operate as a bona fide warm-up for the Kentucky Derby.

John also remembered something his dad had told him when he was a boy. "My dad told me there's no better place in the world to train a racehorse than in Hot Springs. It's quiet, very relaxed, the weather is great, the track is excellent, and the people are out of this world." Training in Arkansas would most certainly be a dream.

"It was no dream...it was a nightmare," John decried. "...at least in the beginning."

John needed Smarty to relax. Smarty Jones just wanted to run. None of the exercise riders could handle him. Pete Van Trump had come with John to Hot Springs, and he had been making some progress; but when Pete went back to Philly, Smarty just had his way with every other rider who attempted to take the reins. Finally, there was one rider who started to work out, "...but Smarty figured him out, too," John chuckled. "Just when this guy thought, I got him...I got him...Smarty said, NOPE...I got YOU...and he was gone again." John was seriously worried that the horse was going to burn himself out. "We could simply not slow him down."

It was right about this time that John got a call from Pete Van Trump. Pete wanted to come back. Pete loved Arkansas; and John knew that if anyone was going to be able to get a handle on his horse...it was Pete. When he got back to Hot Springs however, Pete found Smarty more out of control than ever. "I could still hold him, but I was having a lot of trouble," Pete remembered. "I was holding him so tight...but he was still trying to run. He was actually lunging at times." As far as John was concerned, "that was just as bad as letting him just run by himself without a rider." John was even afraid that Smarty was on the verge of hurting himself.

For the first time in their professional lives, tension was building between the two men. Frustration over their inability to gain the control they needed to have over the animal had caused a temporary loss of focus. John was mad at Pete. Pete was upset with John. They were arguing every day; and the Southwest Stakes was less than two weeks away.

In what few calmer moments existed during this period, the two men discussed equipment changes that they might make; but even here, John wanted to try one device; Pete was opposed. Pete suggested another training aid, and John was not in favor of making the switch. Ultimately, it was agreed that they would roll the dice in the Southwest Stakes and make any changes to Smarty's training regimen, depending on the result.

I was curious at this point, as to whether John ever considered loading up the truck and just heading back to Philadelphia Park. After a long and overly silent pause, John said, "By this time...I knew exactly what I had, and for the life of me, I was going to do whatever it took to make it happen. If we could just get by the first one, I knew we would be okay...I thought we would be okay...I HOPED we would be okay," he laughed.

On the day of the Southwest Stakes, John met with Stewart Elliott to go over his pre-race instructions for his rider. John noticed that "a real nice sprinter" had been entered in the race. The horse's name was Wildcat Shoes, and John told Stew that this horse was "FAST!' He told Stew, "Don't let him drag you around...he's going to be rolling." John knew that Wildcat Shoes would never last the mile.

He told Stew, "...when you're ready to pounce on him, you pounce on him." He also told his jockey, "I don't want you a length off of him all the way around. I want you off of his pace."

When the gate opened, Wildcat Shoes did exactly as John suggested. He broke immediately and made his way to the front. As instructed, Smarty was NOT "a length off of him." Smarty actually trailed Wildcat Shoes by an entire length AND A HALF. John was upset...but not with Stewart Elliott. "It wasn't Stew; it was Smarty. He was FLYING, and Stew just couldn't hold him back."

Things got worse when John saw Smarty tire in the back stretch. "The other horses were running to him... they got about a length from him and he actually took off again...they started to run at him at the wire, and he kicked off again," John said. "That answered the last question I had about Smarty Jones. I always knew he had the talent. Now I know he's got the heart. Now I know he wants to be a racehorse."

Once again, Smarty Jones had won a race. In this instance, his performance was even more impressive to his trainer than that of the previous victories. However, John still came away from the win realizing there was more work to be done. He also knew that he WOULD slow this horse down, and that Smarty Jones WOULD be great. And, for the first time, he didn't mind telling someone about it.

John remembers a local Arkansas Sportswriter, named Bob Yates. Bob had first watched Smarty Jones in the Count Fleet Stakes, before the horse had even reached Hot Springs. Bob loved Smarty, and even after Smarty took up residence in Arkansas, he was still the only racing writer in the region who was writing anything about Smarty.

After the Southwest Stakes, Bob came to see John at the barn. The writer told the trainer that no one in racing, or writing, believed that Smarty Jones could "go the distance." John told Yates to turn off his tape recorder. Off the Record, Servis told the writer, "In three to five weeks, people will be writing about this horse as the next Seattle Slew." A somewhat surprised Bob Yates wanted to know if Servis was serious. A surprisingly confident John Servis replied, "You wait and see how good he gets."

For now, however, it was back to preparing Smarty for the Rebel Stakes...and trying to figure out how to get the horse to settle down.

With three weeks between the Southwest Stakes and the Rebel Stakes, after a handshake and a few beverages of their choice, John and Pete were finally able to agree on what to do to try to get control over Smarty Jones. They would outfit the horse in an apparatus known as a "German Martingale." The technical specifications associated with this device are just boring enough to force even the most patient person to ram a sharp stick into their own eye. However, the operational impact of the training aid appeared to be yet another gift from on high.

According to John, "It was about a week, and he changed (snaps fingers) like THAT! I mean, it was incredible." Smarty went from finishing his workouts sweaty and pounding to being relaxed and at peace with it all. "It was almost like submission for him," John explained. "He would still pull and he still wanted to go, but Pete always had him. He couldn't throw his head up. He couldn't lunge. He couldn't do anything." What he DID, and what John was finally able to do, was get back to the business of molding and shaping this horse into the image that he had for Smarty Jones when the decision was made to come to Arkansas.

The Oaklawn Jockey Club is a beautiful racing facility. It is a grand old raceway which has been owned and operated by the Cella family for over one hundred years. John Servis may not have known this fact when he brought Smarty Jones to Hot Springs. The Chapmans were likewise unaware of the tradition associated with this great racetrack. Team Smarty was also completely unaware that they were on their way to Arkansas at a time when Oaklawn's current owner, C.J. Cella had elected to honor his Grandfather by offering a "Centennial Bonus" to any horse who would win The Rebel Stakes, The Arkansas Derby, and go on to win the Kentucky Derby.

C.J.'s Grandfather had offered a bonus of

$50,000.00, tied to the 1904 St. Louis World's Fair Stakes. One hundred years later, C.J. multiplied that $50,000.00, times the one hundred years since his Grandfather's bonus, offering each and every one of the Rebel Stakes entrants an opportunity to prance out of the Winner's Circle in May, at Churchill Downs, with an additional FIVE MILLION DOLLARS!

Bonuses are routinely offered in all of sports. Golfers can win anything from a new car to a million dollars for a hole-in-one. VISA has offered a Triple Crown Bonus in the horse racing business for the last decade. Companies offering such bonuses derive substantial public relations in connection with the bonus offer.

More importantly, these bonuses are by design, attached to feats of athletic accomplishment which result in the offering entity having little or no concern that anyone will actually ever collect on the bonus offer. In the unlikely event that the Fates do intercede in such a situation and payment on a bonus opportunity becomes necessary, the offering company wins again. The company gets yet MORE public relations value...the athlete is a conquering hero; and of course, some nameless, faceless insurance company actually pays the bonus.

In the case of The Centennial Bonus, apparently C.J. Cella was so not worried about any horse actually collecting on the bonus that he didn't even concern himself with having the bonus insured.

Amazing how something so simple as a

"German Martingale" can change your entire perspective on the proper amount and size of your personal insurance portfolio.

Smarty Jones wasn't the favorite on the day of the Rebel Stakes. He did however, manage to catch the race favorite at the top of the back stretch and go on to win the race by a comfortable three and a quarter lengths. Smarty's winning time was the fastest in the Rebel Stakes in over twenty years. His Beyer Speed Rating of 106 began to attract the attention of at least a few additional local sportswriters. His career record of five starts and five wins, finally landed Smarty a spot on the Las Vegas Oddsmakers listing of Kentucky Derby hopefuls. And, even at 75-1, with one major national racing writer regularly referring to the horse as "Smary Jones," something told C.J. Cella that it was time to find a little insurance for the ol' Centennial Bonus.

The Good News...C.J. found an insurance company willing to get on board.

The Bad News...He could only get two million of the potential five million covered

Chappy had been in the hospital on the day of the Rebel Stakes. He had pneumonia in both lungs. He remembered trying to find a television station that he could get in his hospital room in order to watch the race. Throughout the entire time he was trying to find a station which might be airing the race, he also remembered an earlier conversation he had with John Servis.

After the Southwest Stakes, Chappy started talking to John "seriously" about the Derby for the first time. John told him, "If Smarty wins the Rebel running away, we can start talking about the Derby." After all of the hype, and the highs and lows, the hopes and dreams...Roy Chapman was now laying in a hospital bed unable to see the race, while his son, Michael, relayed a play-by-play account of the event over a cell phone. A smile came upon his face, as Chappy was informed that his horse had just won the Rebel Stakes, "running away."

Not a moment of thought was devoted to bonuses or insurance. It was March 20, 2004. The Arkansas Derby was three weeks away; the Kentucky Derby only three weeks later. Smarty was still an afterthought in conversation between Vegas Oddsmakers and the thoroughbred hierarchy. But, in a Florida hospital, there was smiling. In an Arkansas barn, there was great joy. And, in the heart and soul of a Champion, there was the realization that HIS "mission" was bigger than anything that any of his human handlers could understand, or even imagine.

As the Arkansas Derby approached, local interest in Smarty Jones increased, since he was now the only horse with a chance to win the Centennial Bonus. The national community of racing writers at least began to take note of the horse, perhaps for the same reason. The gang of two-legged entourage members grew in number outside of Smarty's stall. And Smarty...with every breath he took you could hear him simply say, "Let's get it on. I've got a job to do." Smarty Jones was already capturing hearts and minds of virtually all who came in contact with him, and as yet few if any had any idea what he had gone through to get there, how much farther he was destined to go, and were for the most part unaware of the last obstacle which stood in his way.

The Arkansas Derby was important to Smarty Jones for a number of reasons. Of course, it was Step 2 in the process of winning the Centennial Bonus. But, Smarty Jones wasn't born to win the Centennial Bonus. Smarty Jones was born to run, and to inspire, and to change lives; all of which would require Smarty to actually MAKE IT to the Kentucky Derby.

The Kentucky Derby Field is limited to a maximum of twenty horses every year. When more than twenty horses seek to enter, the principal qualifying factor is the amount of money each horse has won in Graded Stakes Races. At this point in his career, Smarty Jones was five starts, five wins and had won nearly one million dollars. However, not a single penny of his winnings had come from a race which would qualify him for the Kentucky Derby.

Smarty Jones would have to win, or finish second in the Arkansas Derby, or the only part of Kentucky he would ever see would be what he saw while looking out of the back of his trailer on his way back to Philadelphia.

The Arkansas Derby drew a crowded field. It also drew much better talent than Smarty Jones had ever gone up against. Smarty Jones drew the outside post position...

...and then the rains came.

John Servis knew Smarty could run. He knew the horse had heart. He had no idea how the weather might interfere his otherwise best laid plans.

When the gate opened, Smarty did what Smarty does best. He broke to the inside, and for the very first time in his racing career, he settled. Two other horses, Purge and Borrego were each properly positioned to win the race. In John's mind, "At the three-eighths pole Espinoza (Borrego's Rider) must have been SURE it was his race." Smarty Jones had other plans. Smarty was two lengths off the pace, and at this point, he put his head down and made his run. "He just ran away from them."

In an amazing stretch run, Smarty Jones had won the Arkansas Derby by one and three-quarter lengths and was now the winner of six races in a row. He was also the winner of a Graded Stakes Race...and he was on his way to Churchill Downs.

C.J. Cella would be on his way to the big dance, too...and hoping to find about three million more dollars worth of insurance along the way.

"When I saw Smarty win the Arkansas...and the WAY he won it, I KNEW I needed to get the rest of the bonus insured. There was no way ANY horse was going to beat Smarty Jones in the Derby," C.J. said.

Both Smarty and C.J. had only three weeks to get their respective acts together.

CHAPTER 7

LET'S GET THIS SMARTY
PARTY STARTED

Whether it is the days leading up to the start of the World Series, the weeks in advance of the Super Bowl, the Countdown to "March Madness," or any one of those anxious moments spent in a waiting room by an expectant father; when something very special is about to happen, you can't even cut the level of excitement with a chain saw. The run up to the Kentucky Derby had provided the world with this kind of energy for 129 years.

While the 130th Kentucky Derby Field continued to jockey for position, with some of the best
"known" three year olds finding out that they had
been eliminated even before the race had begun;
the Smarty Jones Story was now, quite literally,
"Spanning the Globe." Chappy was trying to stay
healthy enough to make it to Churchill Downs. John
was re-shaping the horse's training regimen.
"Smarty Parties" (a concept first initiated by
Smarty's adoptive family at Oaklawn) were being
planned in Pennsylvania, Kentucky, Florida,
Arkansas, California, and as far away as Australia
and New Zealand. All of the media finally cared
enough to spell his name right. And what did
Smarty do?

He slept a lot.

By virtually anyone's assessment, John Servis'
tutelage of Smarty Jones to this point, had been
nothing short of the wisdom and guidance Harry
Potter once received from the immortal Professor
Dumbledor. When he did things the way others did,
John did it better. When he didn't like the way others were doing things, John made a left turn in the
middle of nowhere and blazed a new trail, while the
better-knowns laughed, shook their heads, and
later wondered how John had beaten them all back
to the Winner's Circle.
     The weeks leading up to the Kentucky Derby
again saw John breaking with any number of addi-

tional traditions.

Conventional wisdom suggests that horses and trainers get to Churchill Downs as soon as possible. The horse needs to get used to the track. In the case of a first-time Derby trainer, the trainer needs to get used to the track. More importantly, there are parties to go to; reporters to be stroked and massaged, and all forms of general public relations to be conducted. John would hear none of it. So, while the "A-List" made their customary mad dash to Churchill Downs, John's game plan would be to take Smarty Jones to Keeneland.

"There was an awful lot of construction going on at Churchill," John said. "And there was going to be way too much hoopla. I didn't want any part of it."

Not too many years ago, in any sport at the professional level; winning was simply a matter of your guy going head to head with the other guy, with the best man, woman, or in this case horse, coming out on top. The only "statistic" that mattered was who had the most points, fewest strokes, most goals, most runs, or fastest time when the event was over. Enter the age of computer savvy oddsmakers, professional statisticians, and a whole host of people with just a little too much time on their hands. Now, EVERY sports fan knows the successful third down conversion percentage of an eight man high school football team from Iowa...during away games, played on Thursday, after back-to-back losses, to teams wearing blue jerseys...in October. Somehow I can't imagine ANY-ONE keeping THOSE kind of detailed statistics in connection with thoroughbred horseracing.

You can imagine the look on John's face when the moment he arrived at Keeneland, there was a phone message waiting for him from a member of the Pennsylvania Horsemen's Association.

When John spoke to the gentleman, he was informed that the Pennsylvania Horsemen's Association was concerned about the decision to move Smarty to Keeneland. According to the caller, during an earlier conversation between this caller and a writer from a noted racing magazine, the caller had learned that "no horse has ever come off of the Keeneland Track and won the Kentucky Derby."

This information was soon followed by a suggestion; bordering on an admonishment, that John immediately leave Keeneland and take Smarty Jones to Churchill Downs. Apparently, John was in a bad cell area at the time, however, and the call dropped before John could agree to those terms...

...apparently.

In any event, Smarty was only going to be at Keeneland for a week. John wanted Smarty to just relax and get in a little "down time." As the week wore on, John could tell that Smarty really didn't like the racing surface at Keeneland itself...but he sure did love the atmosphere around the track.

"The whole time we were there, I'd come back to the barn in the afternoon...and that horse would be sprawled out in the stall, sound asleep," John smiled. "That's what I wanted. It was GREAT for him. He loved the place."

Of course it was easy for Smarty to relax, NOW. His win in the Arkansas Derby placed him fifth in terms of Graded Stakes Winnings among the more than twenty three year olds who all shared the same dream. For now however, nap time was over; it was time to get back to work...and on Thursday, April 22, 2004, at 3 PM, Smarty Jones made what amounted to a rather unceremonious first appearance at Churchill Downs.

Notwithstanding the lack of fanfare associated with Smarty's arrival, one veteran national racing writer was moved to remark on Smarty's arrival in this fashion. "Smarty Jones arrived at Churchill Downs, charging off the van as if he were in a hurry to get somewhere." Months later, the same writer would recall his overall experience with Smarty Jones, and remark, "Smarty never WALKS off the van (like other horses). He runs off. It was like he wanted everyone to know, not just that he was there...he wanted them to know that he knew WHY he was there, too."

Smarty left little doubt as to why he was at Churchill Downs. If the rest of the racing world hadn't noticed Smarty Jones before; his first workout at Churchill, on Friday, got ALL of their attention. According to John, "his first workout at

Churchill was ALIVE!" By the end of Smarty's workout, the Backside Buzz had reached deafening deci-
bels. It would be difficult to find space available at
the rail when the horse hit the track for his final
pre-Derby workout on Saturday.

John could tell from the moment they arrived
at Churchill Downs that Smarty "loved everything
about the race track." John liked Churchill, too. He
was very relaxed for someone involved in his first
Kentucky Derby. "Everybody told me to just enjoy
myself and to have a good time," John said. "I tried
to do just that."

And why shouldn't he enjoy himself? Six
months ago, he was a reasonably successful regional trainer with the same dream he had since he was
twelve. Now, he was days away from watching his
colt charge out of the starting gate at the Kentucky
Derby. Smarty had a good first work out. The veteran Derby trainers took to John and were making
him feel right at home. In the words of an oft-refer-
enced beer commercial, "It just doesn't get any better than this." At least not until Saturday.

The Saturday before the Derby would be
Smarty's final workout. His Friday gallop had
turned every head in attendance, and you could bet
there would be a few more heads at the rail to be
turned on Saturday. As usual, Smarty wouldn't disappoint anybody. John called the workout "phe-
nomenal." Steve Haskin, veteran racing writer with
The Bloodhorse Magazine called it, "the greatest
Derby workout I have ever seen." High praise from

a veteran of more than three decades of covering the Kentucky Derby. "He was so smooth, so fluid...I've never seen a horse more together in my life." Jockey Willie Martinez had worked Smarty to :58 for the five furlongs without even a hint of urging. "It's scary to think how fast Smarty might have worked if Willie had asked him for more," Haskin recounted.

Smarty's final pre-Derby workout didn't escape the slightly less than obvious surveillance of the other trainers, either. Later that same day, former Derby winning trainer, Bob Baffert, was asked about a potential jockey change involving his horse, Wimbledon. Baffert responded, "After watching Smarty Jones work this morning...I'm not sure it will make a difference who rides Wimbledon. I'm going to be running for second."

The characteristically inauspicious fates had apparently tipped their hand yet again, demonstrating that not even the Racing Gods could control their exuberance when it came to Smarty Jones.

John had felt pretty good about everything when he and Smarty left Arkansas. "I felt we had a shot," he told me. "An outside shot...but we had a shot." He felt about the same during the week the team had spent at Keeneland. Once Smarty got to Churchill Downs and after seeing the way he nailed that final workout, John began to seriously believe that Smarty could win.

In the week between Smarty's final workout

and the race itself, "Smarty trained great everyday," John said. "I couldn't WAIT for the race to come." John even called his dad and told him, "If he gets beat he's going to have to get outrun...because this horse is ready." John's thoughts turned at this point to the first horse he had ever owned, which his dad had given to him when he graduated from high school; and to the hard road that his father had gone down, first as a jockey, then a jockey's union representative, and ultimately as a racing steward. He was beginning to realize that Smarty Jones "just might win this thing." It was never the "winning" that was important to John; but the thought of his dad not only being proud, but also having a chance to make it to the Derby...and even win, through his son, was very important to this man.

Winning was becoming more and more important to Pat and Chappy, too. The Chapmans had spent most of the pre-Derby period at their home in Florida. They didn't really go out of their way to talk to people about the Kentucky Derby; outside of their own circle of friends, anyway. Privately they thought, "we're just happy to be there...we'll never win." There were competing internal forces at work, however, each operating to play a role in changing the way Pat and Chappy viewed the race, their horse, themselves, and what was happening around all of them.

The Chapmans made their way to Kentucky on the Wednesday before the Derby. Despite the fact that Smarty Jones was the only undefeated horse entered in the Derby, they were met with news article after news article which characterized Smarty as "an underdog" or "a sentimental favorite." "Everybody loves him...but he can't win," the experts had determined. "He doesn't have the right bloodline." Of course, these were the same things that had been said about Smarty since before he hit his head on the top of the starting gate what seemed like forever ago. The difference now, or at least part of that difference anyway, was the fact that Smarty had taken on a gruelling seven week series of three races where he had basically said to the rest of the thoroughbred world, "catch me if you can"...and none of them could.

It was at this point that Pat Chapman felt more competitive urges stirring within her inner self. "It didn't matter what these experts were saying," she said. "Smarty Jones was a gutsy little horse with a big heart."

The origin of the Chapmans newfound desire to win was not replete with selfish interests, a desire to "prove them all wrong," or to seek to enhance their own position in any particular strata or circle; equine or otherwise. While they lived an essentially modest lifestyle, they were financially stable by any standard. Winning or losing the Kentucky Derby wasn't going to change that, at all.

Roy and Pat Chapman wanted to win because, while the experts continued to generate new and improved reasons why Smarty Jones had no shot at winning the Kentucky Derby, the rest of the real world was enlisting in Smarty's Army in numbers which outpaced Uncle Sam on the morning after Pearl Harbor. Letters of support were pouring in from all across the country and from around the world. Smarty was being adopted by schools in numerous regions of the United States. Literally busloads of people were making the trek to Kentucky from Pennsylvania, and Arkansas, and a variety of other locations, just to see Smarty Jones run in the Derby. And, when one of the nation's youngest and more informed racing fans simply couldn't take it anymore, thirteen year old Carly Silver even wrote a letter tracing Smarty's bloodlines, and sent it to Bloodhorse Magazine, as a direct challenge to anyone who would question Smarty's heritage.

The public interest in this burgeoning hero wasn't limited to letter writing, either. "We went to the backside each day that we were at Churchill," Pat said. "You had no trouble figuring out where Smarty Jones was stabled. There were throngs of people everywhere." It was after this outpouring of passion and emotion for Smarty Jones that Pat and Chappy realized that "just getting to the Derby" wasn't good enough anymore. They wanted to win, as Pat put it, "not just for us...but for everyone." "These people were so wonderful...the things they wrote in their letters...the way they reacted to Smarty...I almost felt like we owed it to them, to win."

Smarty's Army seemed to sense even this

commitment on the part of Roy and Pat Chapman, and the rest of Team Smarty, too. A vicious cycle ensued, in the form of a fanatic feeding frenzy. The more the fans gave to Team Smarty, the more they got back. The more they got back, and felt more a part of this extraordinary experience, the more they gave in return. For every handwritten note, card, or letter that Pat, John or Sherry sent out to a fan in the days leading up to the Kentucky Derby, ten new fans appeared from some other corner of the universe with their own best wishes for Smarty and his friends.

There were lighter moments in the days leading up to the Kentucky Derby, too. The area around wherever Smarty was located was always cordoned off, so as to limit direct access to the horse. Everyone associated with Team Smarty was just fine with that situation; everyone except Smarty Jones, that is. The farther the security staff tried to keep people away from Smarty, the more it was HE who tried to gain access to them. "He's such a ham," Pat laughed. "He loved the attention. It was actually Smarty who was trying to get through the security lines so that he could get closer to the people." Even then it was clear that the public loved Smarty; and he was bound and determined to love them right back.

Pat wasn't really laughing though, when she would watch Bill Foster walking Smarty each day. "Bill is so big...he makes Smarty look like a pony," she lamented. "I kept telling them to get someone else to walk that horse. It's no wonder the handi-cappers don't think he can win." Here too, as Bill would walk Smarty, there were times when the two would look straight ahead and just walk. There were also times when Smarty would almost turn to Bill as he continued his walk, absolutely as if he was engaging Bill in some form of conversation. Bill would look back at Smarty, then look back as if in response... Smarty would give any onlookers the now famous Smarty Smile...and you almost KNEW that he had just told his friend, "I'm gonna shock the world in a few days, Pard."

Smarty wasn't the only member of the team taking a beating in the press. With the exception of one Washington Post article which basically talked about the group being "the wrong horse, wrong jockey, wrong trainer, wrong owners," no one really had an unkind word to say about John. And even that particular article was somewhat complimenta-ry in the end...in a left-handed sort of way. Stewart Elliott, on the other hand, was not being afforded the same respect.

Stewart knew most of the other riders, having raced against most of them in the past at various tracks, particularly in New York. But...since the vast majority of the Derby Press Corps was unfamiliar with Stewart, they immediately branded him, "Stew Who." Stew never acknowledged their disrespect. To his credit, he kept himself well-above the com-mentary and just came to work everyday fully pre-pared to do the best job he could do. It bothered

Chappy to no end, though. "It was all you heard all week from those guys (the Press)," Chappy commented. "Stew Who...Stew Who...Well, they sure found out who Stew was," Chappy later said rather proudly.

But, let's not get ahead of ourselves.

CHAPTER EIGHT

MAY 1, 2004

The members of Team Smarty arose on May 1, 2004, still pinching themselves in an effort to make sure that just being in Kentucky that day wasn't a dream. Chappy's pre-race enthusiasm had been generated by John's comments at dinner the evening before. Chappy remembers asking, "Is he ready, John?" John replied, "He's 125 percent ready, Chap...he's a loaded gun." Try getting any sleep at all, after hearing a statement like that from your trainer. "I wasn't being cocky," John stated. "But, I was feeling very good, and I was confident of at least a very good showing."

It would be a long day for the team, regardless of the outcome of the race. Planning and preparation behind them...Smarty's accident not even qualifying as a distant memory; the "wrong horse, wrong jockey, wrong trainer, and wrong owners" were about to make their way to the world's most famous racetrack, to run in the world's most famous horse race...and while they were all clearly the fan favorite, most of the "smart money" remained skeptical. It had been only six months since Chappy told John to "get us to the Derby." For each, the final sixty minutes would seem like sixty years.

There was so much for the entire team to be thinking about, and all they wanted to do was not think at all. It was time to lay it all on the line; time to forget about starting gates, and stumbles, and lunging, and bloodlines, and even fan mail, and just get the job done.

John and Stewart were poised to become the first, first time trainer - first time jockey to win the Derby since 1979. Smarty could become the first undefeated horse to win the Derby since 1977, and only the fifth undefeated Derby Champion in history. Smarty could become only the second Pennsylvania Bred in 130 years to win the Derby. And of course, there was the little matter of a potential five million dollar bonus that had been offered by C.J. Cella.

Speaking of the five million dollar bonus; when last we left Mr. Cella, he was hopping on and off of exit ramps on the road from Hot Springs to Churchill, in search of an additional three million dollars of insurance coverage.

After the Arkansas Derby, C.J. had commented that he knew he needed to get the remaining three million dollars of the bonus covered with insurance because, "nobody was going to beat Smarty Jones in the Kentucky Derby."

This may have been one of those rare times in life when it did not pay to advertise; and where discretion would most assuredly have been the better part of valor. I say this because apparently, even though the oddsmakers hadn't yet climbed aboard the Smarty Express, the insurance companies BELIEVED our good friend Mr. Cella.

As the result of C.J.'s commentary, the outpouring of fan support for the horse, and favorable articles everywhere from the Bucks County Courier Times to the Taipei Times, C.J. Cella simply couldn't find a single pair of "good hands" that wanted to wrap themselves around him...or his bonus. In fact, if C.J. "had a dollar" for every insurance company that rejected his efforts to obtain the remainder of the insurance coverage...he "wouldn't have needed any insurance."

So, when the sun rose on race day, C.J. still stood to be three million dollars on the downside of success by days' end; or at least three million dollars lighter in the asset column of his personal ledger, anyway.

Remember however...strange things happen

in connection with this horse, and the people around him. And, just when it seems as though even stranger things can't possibly happen, of course, that is exactly what does happen. In this case, after not being able to secure additional insurance for the bonus during the weeks leading up to the Derby, C.J. was able to land two million of the three million he had needed to cover, on the very morning of the race, from a foreign insurance carrier. C.J. called Chappy later that same morning to tell him that four million of the five million dollar bonus was now covered. Chappy told Cella that he couldn't care less about the bonus at that point in time. "I wasn't even thinking about any bonus," Chappy said. "This was Derby Day."

C.J., on the other hand was not only still thinking about it...HE was wondering where he would find the other million, in the event that Smarty actually won the race.

More on THIS...in a moment.

It doesn't matter how many times a person has dreamed about driving in the winning run in Game 7 of the World Series. The first time you realize that you are actually at bat, in the bottom of the ninth, with a 3-0 count on you and the bases loaded; your dream becoming your reality right before your eyes, is as overwhelming as actually blasting the next pitch into the cheap seats.

Reality set in, in a big way, and in a rather

abrupt way for John Servis, as he and Smarty Jones headed toward the racetrack on May 1, 2004.

In a group, they left the barn and began the walk which they had made six times together, at three different racing facilities. They had even practiced the same journey here, at Churchill Downs during the previous week. But something was different about today...and it wasn't just that today was May 1st. This wasn't any other racing facility, and it wasn't a practice run. John knew that today, it wouldn't simply be riders, writers and trainers who had come out to see Smarty work. John knew that real people would be there, just as they had for the other thousands of races he had been a part of throughout his career. He simply had no idea how MANY people would be there.

At "the gap" where John and Smarty would enter the track, John found out, exactly how many people he didn't know would be there to see his horse. There was in John's words, "a massive amount of people...at least several hundred people, just lined up as we started into the gap." His dream had become his reality.

"Who Wants to be a Kentucky Derby Trainer?" John Servis did...for his entire life. So what was going through his mind?

"Holy shit," John remembers thinking. "Smarty's groom had the horse's number on his shirt...and as soon as the crowd saw the number, they started screaming, Smarty...Smarty... Smarty." John was walking side by side with his two sons,

Blaine and Tyler. It was the proudest moment of his life, and the one situation from the entire Smarty Jones Experience, which he will never forget.

Tyler, the younger of the two Servis Boys, is a freewheeling, gregarious sort who is comfortable in essentially any surrounding. Older brother Blaine is much more reserved and had not really expressed much in the way of outward excitement in connection with all that was going on around them. This day would be different however, even for Blaine. John's mission in life for the previous three weeks had been to get Smarty Jones to relax; and even with his lifelong dream now about to play out before him, all he could think about was hoping that the pandemonium which was unfolding at that moment wouldn't cause the horse to spook. Even the kids knew this...and as they approached the crowd of people at the gap, Tyler suggested to his father that perhaps it would be better if he could get one of "those signs that they hold up at golf tournaments...you know, the ones that say QUIET PLEASE," and that maybe that way he could help his dad in some small way. Blaine simply looked over at his father and said, "Dad, I am so excited...I can't stand it." John laughed, at least on the inside.

"It really took a lot for Blaine to open up like that," John said. "He's so quiet, and reserved...and I'm thinking...excited, huh? I just don't see it. I was really happy for him to be excited though. Making that walk together, the three of us, at Churchill, with those Twin Spires in front of us...THAT was a special moment for me...for all three of us."

And, in a blink of an eye, literally, John quickly realized that he had far more to worry about himself "spooking" than Smarty Jones. "Smarty was so cool," John remembers. "The other horses were all pacing around in circles. Smarty Jones got to the gap and he just stopped and stood there. He was looking right at the Twin Spires, like he didn't have a care in the world."

"Just looking at Smarty and the way he was acting," John thought, "I knew it was going to be a good day. I felt REALLY good."

Other members of Team Smarty who wished to remain nameless regarding this issue, also recall the walk to the paddock on May 1st. "John was WAY more nervous than Smarty, no question about it," they laughed. John never once admitted that he was nervous, or made a direct comparison between he and his horse, but he did acknowledge that he was "tickled to death" by the level of professionalism exhibited by the animal.

In the paddock, they got a saddle on Smarty and he just stood there like a statue. While he was "amazingly well-behaved" by all accounts, it was something much more than that which caught the attention of all in attendance. Smarty Jones had already begun to make a statement. He stood in the paddock in a way that when you looked at him you couldn't help but notice his confidence. More importantly, he seemed to give those closest to him, as well as all those keeping a watchful eye over him, the idea that he clearly understood that something very special was about to happen...and that he would be at the center of it all.

The biggest beneficiary of Smarty's pre-race attitude, was Stewart Elliott. "You could see that Smarty coming across as relaxed and ready to go as he was, really gave Stew a jolt of confidence," John said. "I told him (Stew), just ride him like you've been. Put him in a good spot...don't move until you absolutely have to. Until then, just sit on him."

John was very proud of Stew as he stood at Churchill Downs handing out his instructions. With the sounds of voices STILL echoing "Stew Who" in the background, John wanted nothing more than for Stewart Elliott and Smarty Jones to have a great ride that day. There were Hall of Fame Jockeys who didn't have mounts in this race, and John could have made a switch and moved any one of them onto Smarty Jones for the Kentucky Derby.

There had been a moment, after the Arkansas Derby when racing writers were all speculating so much about a possible jockey change for Smarty Jones that Chappy went to John and asked, "What should we do about that?" John told Chappy, "We go with the guy who got us here." Chappy asked one more time, and slightly more direct, "On May the 1st, in Kentucky, against the nineteen best three year olds in the world, you're confident that he's our guy?" And, with every bit of confidence, John reiterated, "He's our guy." "Then he's our guy," Chappy said, and there was never another moment of discussion on the matter. Team Smarty would "go with the guy who had gotten them there."

And now, John stood in the paddock at the Kentucky Derby, looking up at his rider and eye to eye with his colt, hoping that both could exorcise a demon or two in the next couple of minutes. For Stewart Elliott, John hoped for redemption; for Smarty Jones...vindication. For himself...he had already experienced a level of joy far beyond anything that he could ever have hoped to be a part of. Win or lose, no one could ever take from John Servis, what the Derby Gods had already given to him, in advance of the Call to the Post.

Fortunately or otherwise, the time to pause and reflect; to second guess yourself, or listen to others do it for you, had passed. "Stew Who" would ride a horse who had nearly killed himself, in a race the "experts" thought neither could possibly win. Post Time, in two minutes.

John was the last person to make his way to the Chapmans' box. By the time he got there, "the place was packed." The horses were in the starting gate; and John and his wife, and Roy and Pat Chapman joined tens of millions around the world as the bell sounded, their hearts pounded, and all of their best efforts were laid upon the table.

Intending no disrespect to any of racing's greatest announcers, listening to John's "call of the race" while sitting in his office months after the Derby had me on the edge of my seat...and I already knew the outcome.

"The gate opens, and he breaks AWESOME," John began. "He put himself in a real good position. The first time at the wire was the most crucial time in the whole race. Smarty's a little tight," John went on. "He's getting bounced around a little, but I'm thinking...he'll try to sprint right off, (I can see John starting to get excited at this point) but he stayed relaxed, held his position, and came out clean." (Now I'M getting excited.) John leaned in, on the edge of his chair, as his play-by-play account continued.

"Down the backside he had a couple horses outside of him...what with the rain, inside is probably the worst part of the track...they were trying to push him in there." John is starting to get really animated now. "Halfway down the backside, Lion Heart is in front by himself. Smarty Jones starts to clear other horses...I know he's fine. Once he cleared them, Stew eased him out." Stew later told John that it was at this point that Smarty JUMPED on the bit.

"I knew we had Lion Heart," John smiled. "Stew knew it, too," he added with that nod of his head that made you know this was a critical moment in his viewing of the event. "The only thing I worried about was what was coming from behind." John said he felt, "pretty good" at this point. "I felt like we were going to get the job done." It was about a sixteenth of a mile from the wire when John realized that Smarty was going to win.

What must it have felt like, in those last few

seconds, when you KNOW your horse is about to win, and before he actually crosses the finish line at the Kentucky Derby? Was it like the ending of a Hollywood movie? Did time stand still? Was there a sense of overwhelming pride or accomplishment; perhaps relief?

"It was more like...YES," John screamed. "I didn't really even have a complete thought. And then...when he hit the wire, it was like...I just won the Kentucky Derby. It was absolutely unbeliev- able," John said (finally taking his first breath). "People in the box are going crazy. I'm thanking Chappy for giving me the opportunity. It was GREAT!" An equally excited Sherry Servis chimed in at this point remembering Smarty chasing Lion Heart at the top of the stretch. "I was thinking, Please, Smarty...just hold on to second. Then Smarty PASSED him and all I could think was, Oh my God...am I dreaming? This can't be happening." A moment or so later she just began repeating, "Dreams can come true...dreams can come true..."

John remembers pumping his fist in the air as Smarty crossed the finish line. "It was weird," he thought. "I don't get excited watching races. It's not my nature. But as Smarty got to the wire, it was like one big flashback."

"I started thinking about Arkansas, the earli- er races, Smarty lunging to break the hold while he was training...Then, after the wire, as he just gal- loped out, it was like someone stuck a pin in me and let all of the air out. The pressure release was so great," John continued. "It's over, I thought...we got it done. You just can't imagine."

It wasn't really "over," however. In fact, the "pressure" that John felt release, would start amassing all over again in just a few minutes once the media onslaught kicked into high gear.

Pat and Chappy were similarly struck at the moment they first realized that Smarty was going to win the Kentucky Derby. "Words can't describe the feeling," Chappy said. "He passed Lion Heart like that horse was nailed to the ground...and you KNEW at that point, he is GOING to win." Pat simply went numb. "My GOD," she remembers saying, almost in tears at the time, "This is our horse." Chappy was across the box from Pat at that specific moment. The place was still a mob scene, now made even less manageable by virtue of the events unfolding on the racing surface. Pete Van Trump was banging into Pat from one side screaming, "He's gonna do it! He's gonna do it!" The minutes seemed like hours, literally, and when Pat and Chappy were finally reunited, in actuality only a short time later, all Chappy could think to say to her was, "Where were you? You hugged everybody but me."

Pat just smiled. She probably should have told him to hold on tight, because their rollercoaster ride was just beginning.

The same construction that John worried about when he decided to take Smarty Jones to Keeneland in the first place, came into play when Roy and Pat tried to find their way to the Winner's

Circle. The crowd at Churchill Downs was at over-flow capacity. Chappy was not allowed to use his motorized wheelchair. For safety reasons, there were no golf carts available. To make matters worse, the police escorts that were assigned to get Chappy to the Winner's Circle walked alongside of his wheelchair, instead of clearing a path in front of him. As a result, not only did the rest of the group have to wait almost a half hour in the Winner's Circle...as did Smarty Jones; but by the time Roy and Pat arrived, "the group" had more than dou-bled in size, and included several dozen people the Chapmans didn't even know.

John was trying to play traffic cop, make sure that Smarty was safe, and insist that no photos be taken until the horse's owners could actually be SEEN in a photo. So much for the pressure being released.

A few thousand quick pix in the Winner's Circle and it was off to the Post-Derby Press Conference. Not surprisingly, one of the first ques-tions asked of the Chapmans, was how it felt to have just won the Centennial Bonus. Somewhat surprisingly, Roy and Pat still had not given the five million dollar prize a moment of thought.

C.J. Cella hadn't forgotten about his bonus. He had a five million dollar obligation, with only four million of it insured. C.J. was out a cool mil-lion...or WAS he?

When C.J. couldn't find a sucker...I mean an insurance company to pick up the remaining million dollars worth of bonus obligation, he made what turned out to be a "sucker bet."

Smarty didn't open the day as the betting favorite, but at some point (perhaps after C.J. dumped a BAG of cash on "Smarty Jones to Win") he became the Post Time favorite, going off at 4 to 1. When Smarty crossed the finish line first, Roy and Pat earned the five million dollar bonus...and C.J. Cella finally found the rest of the money to pay for it. In fact, C.J. made no bones about the fact that his bet on Smarty Jones was what enabled him to pay the full amount of the bonus.

According to C.J., "I even made a little money on the deal." He wouldn't tell me exactly how MUCH money he walked off with after paying the last million dollars of the bonus...but he did say, "Let's just say that I started the day a million in the hole, and ended up with a pretty serious tax problem."

When I reminded C.J. that at the time he made the bet, Smarty Jones was not the race favorite, and that the "smart money" was somewhere else, he responded, "I guess the smart money shoulda been on Smarty Jones, now...don't ya think?"

Then he just laughed, without a doubt...all the way to the bank.

As an aside, I am compelled to close this Chapter with a brief personal comment regarding the owner of the Oaklawn Jockey Club.

Mr. Charles J. Cella is not only one of the

biggest, most dedicated and loyal Smarty Jones fans that I was fortunate enough to happen upon in the course of preparing this book...he is also one of the finest human beings I have been privileged to encounter at ANY time in my life. C.J. doesn't just exude class...he personifies it. From the first thirty seconds of our very first conversation it was glaringly apparent to me, why his family business has withstood the test of time, and why he is looked upon by a wide variety of individuals in and out of thoroughbred racing as a person to be admired, respected and emulated.

My hat's off to you, C.J.

Like Smarty Jones, you too, make this world a better place.

CHAPTER NINE

DEEP BREATH...EXHALE

The 130th running of the Kentucky Derby had been SO surreal for all of Team Smarty that once again, even the day AFTER the event, they were still seeking independent confirmation of the outcome of the race; just to be sure they really won. John's wife woke up, turned to her husband and asked, "Did we win the Kentucky Derby, yesterday?"

Sherry's inquiry was legitimate and found John equally uncertain for the moment, as he made his way to the door of their hotel room. When he opened the door, John found a newspaper at his feet with a huge front page headline that read, "Smarty Jones Wins Kentucky Derby." It was only then that Mrs. Servis said out loud, "I guess we did."

Nine months ago, Roy Chapman asked Mark Reid to "find us someone who can get us to the big race." John Servis didn't just get them to the big race...he had won it for them. While the racing world and some portion of the rest of the world were already talking Triple Crown just about fourteen hours after the Kentucky Derby, (at least in the article he was now sharing aloud with his wife) John's immediate reaction was his own classic half smile, and the realization that it was time to focus on the Preakness.

John's "focus" wasn't immediately committing to run Smarty in the Preakness. His focus was on finding out if Smarty Jones was fine and healthy after his Derby effort, or if he needed a break. Chappy was very excited after the Derby. "You've gotta think Triple Crown once you win the Derby," he said. But John still wanted to work Smarty Jones, at least once before making any promises to run the horse at Pimlico. Chappy and John had actually played their own version of the "WHAT IF" game sometime in advance of the Derby. It was all coming back to John at this moment...even if Chappy was ready to just forget the conversation and make his way to Pimlico.

John remembers grabbing Chappy about a week or so before the Derby and saying, "We need to talk about something very serious." John made sure that Chappy understood that EVEN IF Smarty were to win the Kentucky Derby...if John was not happy with the horse's health or progress, he would not participate in taking Smarty to the Preakness if it would put him in any physical jeopardy, "Triple Crown or no Triple Crown." "We'll be under a LOT of pressure," John told his owner. "The media won't understand or even care why we aren't going to the Preakness. But, I'm just telling you, in advance...if he's not ready, you go without me, or we don't go." Chappy would later acknowledge that the conversation took place, and that he completely agreed with John's sentiments, but also made it clear that having to take a pass on the Preakness would be a major disappointment.

Recalling this prior conversation with Chappy was significant because for the first time really, throughout this entire endeavor, decisions relating to Smarty Jones, would not be the only matters that the members of Team Smarty would be called upon to address. Like it or not...ALL of their lives had changed forever. Smarty Jones was no longer the only overnight success story. The world knew all of their names, and how they all responded to their new found fame, could easily chart the course for the remainder of the journey.

Would this wonderful group of down to earth

people from the wrong side of the thoroughbred racing tracks (no pun intended), be able to maintain the sensibilities which earned them the respect of a city, state, and nation, when each realized that life as they had known it, was gone, forever?

It didn't take John long to realize that things were different. His transition began on the drive from Kentucky back to Philadelphia on the day after the Derby. "We were driving down the interstate, just the other side of Lexington, and this car pulls up beside of us," he said. "There's this guy and a girl in the car and the guy starts screaming and waving. I thought it was cool, at first...but this guy followed us for FIFTY MILES doing that. Cool became a little scary...real fast."

From Pat and Chappy's perspective, they had lived a relatively quiet life up to this point. "Comfortable," by their own acknowledgement, but otherwise, "pretty low key." Now, they would go out to a restaurant for breakfast and the other patrons would spontaneously applaud as they entered or exited the dining room. "People we didn't know would just show up at our house acting as though they had known us all of their lives."

According to Bill Foster, "People would come up to you in the bank, or in a shopping center, shake your hand, and just break into tears. It was unbelievable."

Pete Van Trump likes to tell the story of being on a fishing boat "in the middle of the ocean" (probably not QUITE the middle, I suspect) and the other guy on his boat yells to someone in a nearby boat, "...you see this guy here? He's the rider for Smarty Jones."

There was even a question as to how Smarty Jones would react to the changes which would necessarily attach to his newfound status as the winner of the Kentucky Derby. Well, maybe there was no real issue as to how Smarty would respond to the situation. If there was anyone capable of simply going with the flow; it was Smarty Jones.

Smarty arrived back at his home on the backside of Philadelphia Park, on the Tuesday night following his Derby win. It was, according to John, "pitch black...except for the fact that there were news helicopters, news vans, and news people... EVERYWHERE!" He remembers the camera flashes as "lighting up the entire area."

The other forty-four horses in Barn 11 were upset, and openly showing their displeasure. "Smarty," John said, shaking his head, "...he could have cared less." John thought it was as if Smarty was telling his stable mates, "Here I am, Boys...I'm home." One local news reporter saw it almost the same way. "Smarty stopped after coming out of the van and just stood there like he was Ricky Ricardo announcing to Lucy, that he had just returned home from the club."

So far, it seemed as though at least one member of the team was absolutely taking absolutely everything in stride.

When John left the barn even later that

evening, he made the just over one mile trek back to his housing development to find that each and every mailbox in the complex was adorned with blue and white balloons. There was also an enormous sign congratulating John and his family, which had been erected in their front yard. The Servis family couldn't believe it, but they also were unable to ignore the fact that to people who lived only two blocks away, and had never known them, there was all of a sudden something in the way of an obligation on the part of John Servis to continue to succeed.

Things didn't get any easier for John the next morning either. His first day "back at the office" after the Derby saw at least 150 reporters waiting for him. In the grand scheme of good and bad...this was clearly a bad thing. John had forty-four OTHER horses to work, and still hadn't even made a decision on running Smarty in the Preakness. John was mobbed by the press at every turn, that morning. Every news outlet from Bensalem to Beijing wanted his time. Security at Philadelphia Park was being overrun.

Only seventy-two hours previous, John felt a pressure release that he described as absolutely unbelievable. Now, he felt pressure that was more than equally unbearable.

As John sat secluded to some degree in his office at Barn 11 wondering how he would be able to get ANYTHING done under these circumstances, his wife Sherry Servis was already on her way back from the local Staples Office Supply Store, with a calendar. "In the first hour, I saw what this was doing to him," Sherry said. "I went in to John and told him that this was going to kill him," she relayed. At this point she told her husband, "You just do what you do best, and let me take care of the rest."

In typical John Servis fashion, he WAS trying to be everything, to everybody. He was training ALL of his horses, being the husband and father he had always been, and from even before he returned from Kentucky, doing every interview requested by every writer, radio-tv person, magazine, and any one else who had required a block of his time.

It was at this point, that the usually mild mannered Sherry Servis put her foot down.

There would be no Madison Avenue or Hollywood Public Relations firm coming in to save the day or assist in determining what the meaning of the word "is" is. They didn't want it that way, and wouldn't have it that way. This was an average, everyday wife, stepping up to support her husband, in the same way she had done since the very first day that he was officially dubbed the apple of her eye.

It was also the first and most powerful statement about how the Servis family would react to the course that life had charted for them. They would deal with the things that they could not change...but they would not change themselves, in the process.

After a deep breath, and a sigh of relief, John told me, "Once Sherry got involved, every thing went smooth as silk after that."

John was still concerned that Smarty might need a break, though. At least he felt that way until he saw Smarty train for the first time following the Derby. "He was STILL a monster," John remembered. "It wasn't Smarty who needed a break; it was US. Smarty Jones was just fine."

Team Smarty never got that break. And, even though Smarty may not have needed one, he clearly deserved a break, at least from the writers. Unfortunately, he got no real quarter from the fourth estate just yet, either.

With respect to the Team, Smarty's win in the Derby just seemed to create more obstacles to each doing his or her respective job. John was conducting daily, well-orchestrated press conferences at Philadelphia Park. However, despite the very best efforts of his wife, Cousin Donna, who was also shielding him, and the security staff at the race-track; the entire team was being pushed and pulled at by anyone who could gain any form of access to any of them. None of them were able to escape the ever present eye of some member of the media.

Philadelphia is a very parochial, very close-knit city. To this rule, the in-town media is no exception. Sports are VERY important in this city. From an inner-city hip hop dance championship to the World Series, if a Philly Team is in it...the locals are going to give it more than the attention it deserves in most places, and they are "damn proud of it."

Sure, Philly fans once booed Santa Claus at an Eagles game. It made national news, and to some, is something that the city will simply never live down. The "more informed" Philadelphia sports fan sees it a little differently, however. A real die hard Philly Fan explained it this way. "Yeah, we booed Santa, but hey...the guy was having a bad year, what do you want? He comes up on a contract year, and oh sure, everybody gets what they want...then he gets the fat contract and sits around waiting for somebody else to deliver the presents."

This is the Philadelphia Sports Scene, and an attitude that the local media encourages, is proud of, and capitalizes upon. To the local Philadelphia media, and the average Philly fan who up to this point had no idea Philadelphia Park even existed...Smarty Jones winning the Kentucky Derby was all of a sudden, "PRICELESS."

On the one hand, no member of the local media was any less proud of what Smarty was doing "for the city." In this sense, the sports talk show hosts, sportswriters and TV anchors were no less "fans" than their listeners, readers and viewers. To their endearing credit, as well as their overall professionalism, the local media was able to properly manage the joy and excitement which was circumstantial to the events, with their journalistic obligation to both get, and report on the story. This was NOT to say, however, that the locals were going to let any "outsiders" come in and scoop them on anything.

So, while the scheduled media events went "like clockwork," the virtual nonstop pressure from the local people just wanting to savor the moment in a city starved for a Champion, along with the national and international media trying to muscle their way in, made the days longer than they needed to be, the nights shorter than they should have been; and made it just that much more difficult to get Smarty ready for the Preakness.

There was, however, NEVER even so much as a hint of tension between John, and ANY member of the Press, except for a pushy group of folk from one major national magazine who shall remain nameless. That situation occurred pre-Belmont, and involved people from Newsweek (oops) attempting to bypass the tried and true "Sherry Servis Scheduling System." In point of fact, John had, and has one of the more remarkable relationships with the press, at all levels and in all genres, that has been enjoyed by a major sports celebrity for quite some time. Pat Chapman sees it this way; "From the time John Servis first stepped to the microphone, Roy and Pat Chapman could not have had a better spokesperson."

And, Smarty Jones couldn't have had a better friend or more determined protector.

For some reason however, it didn't seem to matter how cooperative John was with the media. It didn't matter at all that Smarty Jones was STILL undefeated. It didn't matter that he had taken on the best of the best of the best and run away from all of them. Some number of recognized and respected members of the RACING Press were STILL searching for ways to "explain" Smarty's Derby win...followed routinely by a cadre of reasons why he couldn't possibly win the second leg of the Triple Crown. It was the sloppy track, according to some; while others credited Smarty's victory to several horses throwing shoes during the race.

If it bothered anyone on the inside, they never said anything. "All that horse did was win," John laughed. "At some point even the most skeptical writer was going to have to acknowledge that fact." The fans; they were another story, entirely. The fans couldn't give Smarty enough credit, or praise. A good friend from Philadelphia described the week before the Preakness this way.

"Six months ago, Smarty was the Chapmans' horse. Then he went to Arkansas and the whole STATE of Arkansas fell in love with him...Now, he's THEIR horse. As soon as he wins the Derby people are calling him America's Champion. You just wait til after he wins the Preakness and see how many people start claiming some kind of connection to him. You won't be able to squeeze another gnat onto that bandwagon."

In truth, my friend was only partially correct. Even before the Preakness, the "Battle for Smarty Jones" was already in full swing.

For the record, Philadelphia Park is not actually located in Philadelphia. Philadelphia Park is located in Bensalem, Pennsylvania. "Ben Shalom" to some of the long time locales; an unlikely linguistic nightmare ("Is that one word, or two?") to 411 operators and telemarketers; Bensalem is a blue collar suburb of Philadelphia which sits just across the northeastern most border of the larger city. In the past, the two governmental entities have battled over tax revenues, economic development and other more traditional political situations and circumstances.

Now however, a week after the Kentucky Derby, both had officially laid claim to Smarty Jones. Joseph DiGirolamo, the Republican Mayor of Bensalem, and John Street, the Democratic Mayor of Philadelphia were both issuing Proclamations honoring Smarty, and declaring him to be "theirs."

Was Smarty Jones "The Pride of Bensalem?" Or, was he "The Real Philly Flyer?" Don't ask Pennsylvania Governor Ed Rendell to weigh in on this internal dispute ...he was hard at work preparing his OWN Proclamation which sought to officially designate Smarty Jones as "Pennsylvania's Horse" (a measure which had broad-based, bi-partisan support in the state capitol, I might add).

Nor would the State of Arkansas be outdone during this first week after the Kentucky Derby. On Monday, C.J. Cella made his way to Philadelphia Park to formally present the Chapmans with an oversized check for five million dollars, and effecting the largest bonus payment in the history of

Smarty Jones, with Stewart Elliott aboard, breaks clean in the 2004 Southwest Stakes, at the Oaklawn Jockey Club.

Smarty cruises to victory in the
2004 Southwest Stakes

Pete Van Trump, John and Smarty
are all smiles (finally) while training in Arkansas.

Lucky Seven brings it home again
in the 2004 Rebel Stakes

According to John,
"Smarty just LOVED to read articles written by people who
doubted him. He got a big kick out of it."

Smarty's Groom, Mario Arriaga
shows horse and rider the way to the Post
at the 2004 Arkansas Derby.

Stew and Smarty (far right)
have a long way to go to get to the rail in the
2004 Arkansas Derby.

SMARTY DOES IT AGAIN...
crossing the finish line first and winning the 2004 Arkansas Derby.

Mario, Stew and even Smarty sport their own smiles
after winning the 2004 Arkansas Derby

John, Roy Chapman (seated), Pat Chapman (center)
along with John's Family and the rest of Team Smarty
receive congratulations from Oaklawn Jockey Club Owner, C.J. Cella
after Smarty's 2004 Arkansas Derby win.

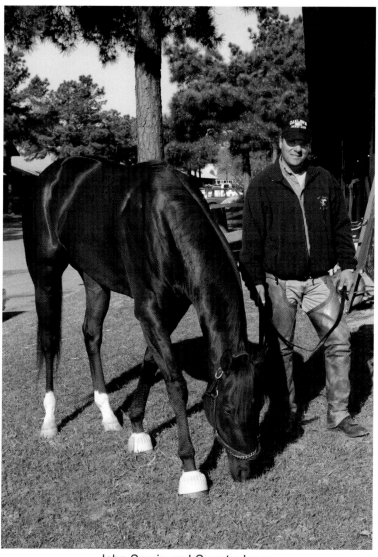

John Servis and Smarty Jones
discuss racing strategies and philosophy of life
in advance of the 2004 Kentucky Derby.

Smarty Jones cruies to victory
on May 1, 2004
in the 130th running of the Kentucky Derby

The VERY crowded Winner's Circle
following Smarty's Kentucky Derby win.

Thumbs UP!!!

Smarty enjoys a little quiet time
in advance of the 2004 Preakness.

Nearly 20,000 stand in line for hours,
just to see Smarty Jones at his last public gallop.

Back to work.
Smarty Jones runs away from the field in the 2004 Preakness,
at Pimlico.

Smarty crosses the finish line,
11 1/2 lengths ahead of his nearest competitor
to set a new record for the largest margin of victory
in the 129 year history of the Preakness.

The dream continues for Roy and Pat Chapman.

Smarty and best friend Bill Foster
swap stories as the two prepare for a
date with destiny.

With more fanfare than a typical Head of State,
Team Smarty
makes its way to Belmont Park.

The dream becomes a nightmare.
Smarty Jones is passed by Birdstone
in the final ten seconds of the 2004 Belmont Stakes.

North American Thoroughbred Racing. Originally, the presentation of the Centennial Bonus had been scheduled to be made at Oaklawn, however, C.J. volunteered to bring the check to the Chapmans in Pennsylvania, in order to alleviate any concerns over Chappy traveling while in poor health. As a result, Smarty's home crowd was able to bear witness as the bonus was presented, making Smarty's Kentucky Derby payday, the single largest payout to a horse in the history of the sport.

In recognition of Smarty's accomplishments, and of course, because he is also "Arkansas's Horse," Governor Mike Huckabee of Arkansas issued his OWN Post-Kentucky Derby Proclamation on Friday of the same week, declaring the day, "Smarty Jones Day," throughout the Razorback State.

WOW! Not a bad week for Smarty. Not only did he earn the largest payday in racing history; he also got adopted by one local Township, the fifth largest City in the United States, one State and one Commonwealth. He also participated in a very rare public workout for his fans.

It had been announced that on May 8, 2004, fans would be given an opportunity to enter Philadelphia Park early, in order to watch Smarty gallop. On this day, very early in the morning, hours before the two thousand or so regular Saturday betting populous would appear, anyone who wanted to see Smarty go through his morning ritual would be permitted to do so. For his part, Smarty wasn't going to be doing anything special, just another jog for him. In fact, he and John were already out on the track and well into the routine when, "all hell broke loose."

"I was on the pony, and Pete was up on Smarty," John said. They were out on the track, just going the wrong way and not doing anything particularly special. As the two made their way past the seven-eighths pole, apparently, the doors to the park had just been opened to the public. "Those people came CHARGING down to the rail," John said in amazement, "Smarty actually got a little surprised by it. Then, when we came back around and saw ALL THOSE PEOPLE...it was unbelievable!"

John wasn't the only person to suggest that he had never seen anything like this before. Lance Morrell, head of security at Philadelphia Park commented, "Every time I think that I have seen everything, something else happens." Lance's comments were understandable, given the fact that a very conservative estimate put the early morning crowd at well in excess of five thousand, with at least one estimate as high as eight thousand. Keep in mind that on a GOOD weekend day at Philadelphia Park an entire card of racing may draw less than two thousand through the turnstiles.

These fans got what they came for, too. On Smarty's second pass by the crowd, he held his head high, arched his back and just RIPPED down the track with the look, feel, sense, and even the smell of a Champion.

Fans also got their first real opportunity to formally participate in "Smarty Mania" through the purchase of all things Smarty. Inside the park, one stand had been set up to sell "Officially Licensed" Smarty products, such as hats, shirts and a few other items. The moment the doors to the park opened, the single souvenir stand was "gang-stang," with ALL of its' items gone in a shorter period of time than it had taken Smarty Jones to capture the Kentucky Derby Trophy.

Outside the park, everyone with "green" was buying ANYTHING that was "blue." Park Security, with the aid of local police were chasing off one unauthorized vendor after another, until at some point fans who simply wanted to get their hands on whatever was being offered, themselves began to hassle the authorities and side with the purveyors of everything from buttons to cd's, pennants to t-shirts, and much, much more.

To Smarty, this was just another morning rip and run. To Philly Park executives it was a market-ing windfall. To the local authorities and Park Security it was "just wrong." But, to the fans who had waited in line since as early as 4 AM, it was 1980 all over again. In THAT year, Philadelphia was "The City of Champions," with nearly all of its' pro-fessional sports teams either winning, or at least participating in the championship game in their respective sports. Today, as a group, a new "Champion" was crowned, and he was every bit as much "theirs" and they were every bit as proud of him, as they had been of "their" Phillies, Eagles, Flyers and Sixers, of twenty-plus years ago.

Almost as if it all had taken place in the blink of an eye, which is not entirely that far from reality; the morning gallop was over. Smarty was on his way back to the barn for a well earned sponge bath, while a gaggle of regional politicos were yet again in search of new and improved ways to capitalize on something that none of them had anything to do with. The single bright and shining light in all of it; Sherry Servis. She wasn't going to get caught up in where Smarty lived, who HIS political representatives were, or weren't, and whose horse he was, or wasn't. When Sherry was asked to address the gathering, she opened by telling the crowd how fortunate that Team Smarty was to have the people of both "Bensalem AND Philadelphia" as fans, and cheering them on.

In case you were wondering what any of this has to do with a Chapter entitled, "Deep Breath ...Exhale," it is simply this. In the span of two minutes in Kentucky, on May 1, 2004, at least a dozen lives changed forever. The people who were there at the beginning, and would be there at the end, whenever the end might come; were now "responsible" for more, not only than they had ever bargained for in life, but for more than anyone in their position woulda, shoulda, or coulda been able to accept.

The same offering, of fame, fortune, notoriety, and the like is afforded to average individuals who become involved in some way in sports, entertainment, politics, or any other field where your profession puts you in the public eye, not by choice, but simply by virtue of your participation in that particular endeavor.

More than a few such individuals have abandoned the principles which accompanied them on the road to that success. More than a few such individuals immediately saw themselves as not only bigger than the game, whatever the game may have been...but to have actually become the game.

Team Smarty no longer represented themselves, or even their horse. At the very least, Team Smarty represented a city that would float a municipal bond to obtain a sports champion. They represented an entire racing industry which had tried for decades and failed to bring new blood into the sport. They represented a nation which had been ripped apart in recent years, and given the political climate of the country could not find a single thing which even so much as a true majority of America could rally around. They represented a coming together that was sorely needed, in and out of sports. And, in the face of the first legitimate challenge to the principles which brought this opportunity to them in the first place, as an entire group, this remarkable collection of unlikely heroes held true to all that it was, in which they believed.

With one down...and two to go, Team Smarty had taken its' deep breath...exhaled, and was on its' way to Pimlico.

Champions already, all of them, in pursuit of perfection; because of their openness, honesty, reality, and understanding, we were able to share each day as if we were somehow truly a part of the experience.

CHAPTER TEN

PREAKNESS 2004

In the same manner in which John had been in no hurry to get Smarty Jones to Churchill Downs prior to the Kentucky Derby, he was even less anxious to bring Smarty to Pimlico in advance of the Preakness.

Unlike Churchill, where John had never raced, but was more than aware of the ongoing construction issues; he had raced at Pimlico, and was acutely aware of the backside accommodations. "It's just not a good setup," John said. "The press is able to get right up on top of you, and the security isn't like what we had been used to at Philadelphia Park. We knew what we had at Philly Park, and we liked it, so there was no sense in leaving any earlier than we had to."

The team would finally "have to" leave their safe haven on the wednesday before the Preakness. Unlike his arrival at Churchill Downs, which had been described as, "without fanfare," Smarty's arrival at Pimlico came at 12:48 pm on May 12, 2004, and was this time heralded as, "much anticipated."

The Chapmans didn't leave for Pimlico until the Friday before the race. Their daughter, Donna, had been trampled by a horse earlier that morning, and they didn't even want to attempt the trip until they were certain that she was in good health. After being released from the hospital later that day, Donna was able to drive to Pimlico with her brother. In a sense, Donna's injuries put something of a damper on the event for the family; but on the other hand, Pat would later be treated to a surprise visit by her other daughter, making the Preakness the only one of the three Triple Crown races which would be attended by all five of the Chapman children.

Pimlico also had a special place reserved in

the hearts of Pat and Chappy; one that they had completely forgotten about until the day of the race itself. While they were waiting to go to the temporary saddling area in the infield, the Chapmans remembered that the first horse they ever ran, was out of Pimlico, a horse named "Small Victories." That, was quite some time ago, and seemed even longer as they stood in the same location hoping for what would be the biggest victory they might enjoy as of yet.

John had scheduled only light workouts for Smarty on Thursday and Friday, along with a little schooling at the starting gate. John wasn't entirely sure where things were with Smarty, since he hadn't really worked him, but he "felt good about everything."

The supportive arm of the press was still being supportive. The detractors were suggesting rather strongly that all of the conditions were right for Smarty to finally meet his match. The racing pontificates even took after John to some degree in this instance, as well. "How could he not even fully work Smarty before the Preakness," they queried. "Why did he wait so long to bring the horse to Maryland?" In the days leading up to the race, it almost seemed as though some of the writers were using their daily columns, and the questions they were raising regarding John and Smarty, to set up what they either thought, or perhaps hoped would make a great headline in the event that Smarty Jones did not win the Preakness.

The fans...their numbers just kept growing, and growing, and then growing a little larger. To John, it seemed as though he was being asked the same questions over and over, and if the answers he gave weren't exactly what someone wanted, they rephrased a question in such a way as to allow him to repeat the same answer, only this time to have it deemed to be just what the interviewer was hoping to get from the meeting. In his mind, there was really nothing left to say, other than "go" and see who wins.

When it came time for pre-race instructions, this day, John was not nearly as detailed as he had been in his admonishment to Stewart Elliott in advance of the call to the Post at Churchill Downs. "Just do what you do best," John counseled his rider. "Go get your picture taken." For some as of yet unknown reason, John felt no pressure at all at that moment. Or perhaps he did, but he internally harkened back to the confidence he saw generate on Stewart's face in the Derby paddock, when Smarty Jones made it appear as though HE had everything under control.

Either way, John is both decidedly superstitious, and generally a creature of habit, so there was no way he was going to make Stewart think that there was anything other than a great ride in his immediate future.

There was something even more mystical about this day than any other day in which Smarty had made his way onto a racetrack. The tension in and around the racing facility was extraordinary. At the same time, there was a calm, at least among the members of Team Smarty, unlike anything that they had experienced over the last several weeks.

John thought to attempt to explain away the lack of anxiety by suggesting that Team Smarty had really already achieved what they had set out to accomplish. They had won the Kentucky Derby, so anything else would be icing on the cake. No need to be nervous. But, how can you not be anxious or nervous, in light of the fact that while you may have accomplished your ORIGINAL goal; you NOW represent "The World" and are responsible for the hopes and dreams of an entire worldwide community of people who want more? How can you not become even just a little anxious when the moment Smarty hit the track for the Post Parade, a roar went up from the crowd, as if the horse had just crossed the finish line?

There were nearly 113,000 people in the stands, and from the crowd reaction the second Smarty appeared, you just knew that even those who had already bet against him, were pulling for Smarty Jones, to win. This was clearly a special day.

If I enjoyed any one thing in the course of performing the research in connection with this book, it was listening to John Servis talk, not just about this horse...but about each race, as well. John is like a walking recordable DVD player, with at the very least, virtual surround sound, when it comes to his recollection of each and every race. Who needs an eidetic memory, when you have access to John Servis. I had to chuckle myself, at times...especially when John would tell me how little time he had on any given morning or afternoon; and believe me, he IS a busy man...but would then go on to talk about, especially the races themselves, as if absolutely nothing else had to be accomplished that day.

As we started into our consideration of the running of the Preakness, the calmness with which John employed in order to outline his pre-race chat with Stew in the Pimlico paddock, was replaced, rather rapidly, with the up on the edge of his seat, here we are re-living the event all over again manner in which he related to me, Smarty's Kentucky Derby ride.

"Smarty Jones just went out and ran an OUT-STANDING race," John began. "When he made a move to the inside in the middle of the turn and went to the inside, I'm thinking, OH NO, he's gonna get squeezed...but then, he just got through there so easy, and I saw Rock Hard Ten running...I could tell Stew had a lot of horse left," he almost cackled. "Then Smarty just shifted gears and WENT. A six-teenth of a mile from the wire, I KNOW I got a BIG SMILE on my face. Right then I was thinking, after the Derby, writers wrote that it was a fluke and how the slop helped him...well...how are they going to explain THIS one away?"

It was at this point that I really wanted to know if the pre-race exhibition of confidence in the paddock was real, or if it was just something that he thought would keep Stew, and/or Smarty Jones in the right frame of mind. "Did I think he could win," John quizzed. "Yeah...I thought he could win...but by eleven and a half lengths," he mused with almost his own aura of disbelief. "No way. I didn't expect that at all. That surprised the hell out of me."

Winning by the largest margin in the history of the Preakness, the Chapmans had a little longer to let Smarty's win sink in before their horse got to the wire, too. Pat and Chappy both said that at the far turn was when they realized that no one was going to catch Smarty Jones.

Chappy acknowledged that the sight of Smarty all alone and running for daylight brought tears to his eyes for the first time throughout the eight races in which Smarty had been entered. "He ran one HELLUVA race," Chappy said, fighting back the very same tears, yet again. "He just went out there, and blew those other horses off the track."

Pat wasn't sure she could recall her immediate reaction to realizing that Smarty had done it again. In Kentucky, she said she had felt numb as a result of the experience. In Maryland, she felt like she had not only gone numb once more, but that she had basically "shut down."

Eleven and a half lengths can seem like an eternity at times; especially when numbness has shut your life partner down, and the only thing you can think about is, "here we go again...how in the hell are we going to get to the Winner's Circle?" I guess that's what they mean when they say "heavy is the head that wears the crown," or in this case, the black-eyed susans.

There was a lot about this particular race that wasn't like the last one, for the entire team. Smarty's training schedule and structure was totally different. The Chapmans managed to have all of their children with them to witness the event. John was less guidant than he could remember in his pre-race dealings with Stew. The weather was perfect...and Smarty Jones just went on and, as John described it, "did what he did best."

John told Bob Yates before the team had even left Arkansas, that in a very short time people would be writing about his horse in the same context as Seattle Slew. After Smarty's runaway, record setting victory in the Preakness, many of those writers were about to start writing about Smarty Jones in the same sentence as the great Secretariat...and in just about the time period that John had first suggested.

The 129th running of the Preakness was complete. Another Chapter in the Smarty Jones Story had been written without the single stroke of pen or key. A significant majority of the 112,688 fans in attendance openly wept. A sportswriter might have referred to the crowd as "112,688 racing fans in attendance," but many of them weren't even "racing fans." Many in the gathering were just "fans." They were fans of Smarty Jones "the horse" or even "the person" and not just Smarty Jones, the racing phenomenon.

The tears were shed not because forty cents was won on a two dollar bet. The tears were shed because these people wanted something from their hero, and he gave it to them. He gave willingly, and in a form and fashion that amounted to a record setting performance on his part. And, he gave it in a way that couldn't help but to cause even the most committed former skeptic to take notice, and rethink his own position.

Hall of Fame Jockey, Gary Stevens, who rode Rock Hard Ten to a second place finish opened his post-race remarks by saying, "I had another gear left...but Smarty Jones had four more." Stevens went on to state, "That horse is as good as any horse I have ever seen, and I have seen some good ones, and I have been on some good ones. Smarty reminded me of Secretariat the way he pulled away."

Trainers and others who rode in the race that day chimed in with their thoughts on what had made the ride, and the day so special. Ken Schanzer, President of NBC Sports commented on the tremendous TV Ratings for the Preakness by saying, "This is a tribute to the popularity of Smarty Jones." One noted racing writer asked if there was any doubt, "that divine forces are guiding this remarkable colt and his supporting cast of characters," and the least known perhaps of all of that cast, Smarty's Groom, Mario Arriaga just said after the race, "My heart go boom, boom, boom." John's wife confirmed the existence of the same divine intervention when she said, "When I saw Smarty hit the stretch all alone, there wasn't just the realization that he was going to win...I knew for the first time that this was a gift from God. It was the first moment that I thought, we might really win the Triple Crown."

Sherry Servis went on to describe her own brand of amazement at Smarty's success in general. "As I watched Smarty heading to the finish line at Pimlico, so far ahead of the others, I kept thinking ...he's this little red horse. He looks so small, and then they put the tack on him and he just transforms...you know, like those old toys, the Transformers, and all of a sudden, he becomes a super hero...and he can do anything." I loved listening to Sherry Servis this day. Her emotion and passion, her sincerity and basic internal honesty...all of it flowed in the same manner as if she had been reading from one of the hundreds of thousands of letters to Smarty that had already been received up to this point...and these were her own words; right from the heart.

Still, for all of the pre-race hype, hoopla and media attention after the Derby and in advance of the Preakness, and all of the headache that it caused to the various members of the team, their ability to relax as they did, on race day, and the way they all responded to now being less than three minutes away from certain immortality, was like nothing that I have ever seen in sport.

At the Derby, John pumped his fist in the air

when Smarty crossed the line. Today, he smiled, and hoped that his group would not need a reservation at the Crab Shack that he wanted to take them to when they were finally able to get out of the racetrack. At the Derby, Chappy was about as excited as a dreamer can get, when his dream comes true. Today, he shed a tear and worried about how to get his family to the Winner's Circle while there was still room for all of them in the picture.

One time, each year...one horse has a chance to move to within one step of accomplishing a feat that has eluded all but eleven, in the history of thoroughbred racing. Yet Team Smarty, as a whole, was both loosier AND even goosier, than at any time during the process, at least this day, anyway.

It probably wouldn't stay that way for the three week period between now and the moment of truth at the Belmont Stakes...but, from a writer's perspective that was AOK by me because, it's in times like these, when people are most relaxed, that some of the really funny stuff happens.

For employees of VISA, please skip ahead to Page 135. The rest of our readership is about to share a reasonably significant "guffaw" somewhat at your expense.

For nearly a decade, the races which make up the Triple Crown have been sponsored by the good people at VISA. Ask virtually anyone in the horse business and they will tell you that when it comes to sponsorship, the people at VISA go "all out" in their effort to take excellent care of the participants in each race, and always make their VISA Triple Crown experience one which they will never forget. There are parties, "Goodie Bags," freebies in various forms, all of which are designed to take maximum advantage of what is by any relevant standard, a major advertising and marketing commitment on behalf of the company. Oh, and of course, there is the FIVE MILLION DOLLAR "VISA TRIPLE CROWN BONUS."

I think by law, I was obligated to put the reference to the bonus in "all caps" because even though the bonus is one which has been offered since the VISA sponsorship has been in place, AND, oh by the way...is fully insured in the unlikely event of either a) a water landing, or b) lightning actually striking for the twelfth time in racing history; (in which case VISA will get even more press without having to actually foot the bill for the bonus on its' own)... still it IS a huge bonus, and THIS is the kind of positive public relations any company making this investment, would expect to receive in return.

As an added benefit to participants in the three races, VISA also provides each jockey and trainer with complimentary SUV's for their use during the week previous to each race. In advertising, this is what is known as a "cross-promotional opportunity" and allows another company to participate in VISA's exclusive sponsorship, while sharing some of the expense, reducing VISA'a ultimate cost of the sponsorship, and in this particular case, the car company then draws a little post-race benefit by being able to later sell the SUV's, presumably at a premium, because people might pay a little more for a truck that had been "USED AT THE PREAK-NESS," for example, "BY JOHN SERVIS."

As we are aware by this time, Smarty Jones did win the Preakness, and did so in record fashion. We know that a record crowd of 112,688 people watched from the stands at Pimlico, along with enough TV viewers to make the telecast of the race the highest rated Preakness since 1990. We know that betting on the race soared to in excess of 85 MILLION DOLLARS, also a record, and that more press credentials were requested and issued for the race, than for any of the previous 128 runnings of the event.

Little has been written however, about the experience that John Servis was forced to endure in order to actually get out of the racetrack that afternoon.

There is an endearing quality to John Servis. He's honest. He's down to earth. He's really a genuinely nice guy. Anyone who has an opportunity to make his acquaintance can see that right off the bat. He's the kind of guy that if you don't know him, and only see him on television, you want to get to know him. Add a dose of Smarty Mania to the equation; in this case, Smarty having just won the second leg of the VISA TRIPLE CROWN, and it is not hard to understand why on this day, the fans simply did not want their time in John's company to end.

After the race, the gathering in the Winner's

Circle, the Press Conference, and the onset of mass hysteria, John attempted to make his way out of the facility, only to find himself being followed by throngs of overly energized fans, now quite some time post-race, but who in almost Pied Piper-esque fashion, just wanted to be close to John while they continued to chant "Smar-ty, Smar-ty, Smar-ty." John did, as John always does, he smiles and gets a little caught up in the natural excitement himself, and sincerely appreciates "the roar of the crowd."

All of that being said, at this point in the day, John just wanted to get out of the track and get to the Crab Shack where he and his family and friends had planned a relaxing evening. With the aid of a police escort, and after another few hundred auto-graphs to the last of the Pimlico faithful, John was FINALLY able to find his way out of the building. John and his only brother, Jason, were now safely ensconced in the complimentary SUV which had been provided by VISA, and would soon be headed back to their hotel and ultimately, on their merry way...IF they could get the ignition on their truck to unlock, that is.

"Here we are, TRYING to get back to the hotel," John said, "and we canNOT get the ignition on this truck to unlock, for nothing."

According to John, "We tried EVERYTHING!" They pushed things...and pulled things...and as frus-tration set in over the course of a few minutes, they BANGED a few things. Actually...the truth be known (which it obviously is, now, haha), they banged

QUITE a few things. As the minutes passed and the frustration level approached whatever stage it is that is one step beyond critical mass, the banging might have been described by an untrained observer; as tag-team, tandem, or even "stereo," as both John and his brother did their best to "forcibly" unlock the truck's ignition and steering column.

There was a moment however, a personal epiphany if you will, (and as you KNOW there always is) when a pause was taken; just long enough for John's brother to ask, "Hey John...where are the Programs that I put in here?"

As we have ALL DONE, when we have ALL told the story where WE have been in this situation, we NEVER just say, or even perhaps whisper, "P.S., we were in the wrong truck." In classic fashion, at first blush, John skipped that part and went right to the explanation portion, of the story, as well. "Man, I'm telling you...it was the same color. It had the VISA logo thing on the side and everything..."

We were both still laughing pretty much uncontrollably until I asked if he had any idea whose truck they were actually in at the time of the "vehicular assault." "I don't know whose truck it was," John said, still concerned enough to literally look over both shoulders to see who might hear, "but we beat that thing up pretty good, trying to get it to unlock."

There was further comedic and yet cosmic irony abounding in Maryland that day, also. The Servis Family turns out to be every bit as superstitious at every level. John really does own more than one jacket, he simply elected to wear the same one at every race, because somehow it either made Smarty run faster, kept the other horses too busy chuckling to catch Smarty, or provided Smarty with some super secret advantage of which we may never be made aware. Sherry's entire closet is not black and white. She does possess clothing of color. She is however, convinced that when Smarty sees her in anything black and white...he will let nothing stand in his way to get to the Winner's Circle. Even Sherry's brother-in-law, Dallas, refuses to do anything differently, once a winning streak has begun.

When Smarty started to win, Sherry's brother-in-law placed a $100 wager to win on Smarty, and because he won THAT race, Dallas felt compelled to make the bet in each subsequent race. In truth, up until the Preakness, Sherry had actually been making the bets for her brother-in-law; but this day, in addition to the bet Sherry had made for him, Dallas decided to place an identical bet on his own. He went to the window, and told the teller he wanted to wager $100 "on the Number 7 horse, to win." After Smarty won his race, Sherry's brother went to the window to collect his paltry winnings.

The bad news...Sherry's brother-in-law made his wager before the TENTH RACE (two races before the Preakness) and he did not specify that he wanted his bet on the Number 7 horse IN THE TWELFTH RACE. So, in reality, he had wagered his

$100 on the right number...wrong race.

The good news...NUMBER 7 WON THAT
RACE, TOO! And, at significantly longer odds;
making the payday more than a little something to
write home about.

So much for the comedy, but what about that
irony we had previously mentioned? The horse who
won the Tenth Race that day was named Gators &
Bears. Gators & Bears was a horse which had been
bred by Bob Camac, Smarty's original trainer who
was murdered by his step-son, Wade Russell.

Gators & Bears was out of a mare by the
name of I'll Be Along. Smarty Jones, of course, is
out of a mare by the name of I'll Get Along.

Pat Chapman had proclaimed on numerous
occasions throughout the course of the Smarty
Jones Journey that she "just KNEW" that Bob
Camac was somehow along for this ride. Chappy
suggested that perhaps Bob was keeping an eye on
his investment. Apparently, at least this day, he was
keeping an eye on Sherry's brother-in-law's investment, as well.

Trucks trashed, winning tickets cashed, soft
shell crabs washed down with just enough of the
beverage of their choice to make the reality of it all
go away, John and Sherry prepared to head back to
Philly Park and try to make it through what would
undoubtedly be the most difficult three weeks of
their lives.

Despite the incredible success that their horse was enjoying, Pat and Chappy weren't holding up as well under the intense media pressure as they would have liked, and would just prefer that the next three weeks get over with no further input from them. In fact, Chappy's parting words to the record breaking number of journalists who covered the Preakness made his intentions more than clear. "No disrespect to you guys," Chappy said, "You've all been great, but my wife and I are going to be taking up residence in Nome, Alaska for the next three weeks."

What was Smarty thinking about the events which would play out over the next three weeks? Who knows. He was sprawled out in his stall at the time, wearing his classic "Smarty Smile."

Some things never change.

CHAPTER ELEVEN

THE BEST OF TIMES

For all of the complaining, pseudo-complaining, threats to move entire families to Alaska at least temporarily, and the like; the three week period between Smarty's record-breaking Preakness victory and the Belmont Stakes would be the single most exciting period in the lives of the members of Team Smarty.

Sure...John would have to take time out of his already media enhanced schedule to be recognized and honored at Philadelphia Phillies baseball games, and Philadelphia Flyers Stanley Cup hockey playoff games. No matter; John is a huge sports fan in general, and quite the "homer" in his own right.

Okay...so there were the school classes who interrupted the daily training ritual and appearances to be made at classrooms and assemblies as far away as John and the Team could drive and still be back in time to make whatever nightly media events were planned. But hey...it was "for the kids," and John made it clear very early on in this process that bringing enjoyment to children through these pursuits, was every bit as important as winning races.

And, then there were the people who would simply show up at the barn. "I'd be sitting in the office and get a call from the guard shack," John said. "So and so is here to see the horse, the guard would say...I would ask who they were, and it turns out...they were just people driving down the road thinking that they could drop in and say hi to Smarty Jones. It was unbelievable."

As "unbelievable" as the thought of making a casual and very unannounced visit to the home of the world's most popular sports icon may actually be; the even MORE unbelievable "result" was that John customarily advised the guards to "send 'em on over" and proceeded to give the people a fifty cent tour, which included having a gander at their hero. Earlier on in this work, I was compelled to stop for a moment and ask a series of "WHAT IF" questions. Another came to mind as John related this portion of the story.

WHAT IF, for example you just happened to be in Chicago for a day, at about the time that the Chicago Bulls were preparing for the final game of their fifth straight NBA Championship, and you thought, "hey...why don't we stop in and say hi to Michael Jordan?"

How long do you think it would take the police to haul you away from Tiger Woods front door?

What are the chances of Barry Bonds responding favorably to you just showing up at his home?

John almost always responded favorably. He almost always brought the people in, was more than a little courteous to them, and gave them a chance to see the horse. Smarty didn't seem to mind either. "He was always on," Maureen Donnelly laughed. "He loved being around the people, and he could sense that they were just happy to see him, too. Besides, Bill was always there, just in case anybody got out of hand."

Bill (Foster) was "always there." Since before the Derby, Bill had basically lived in the barn and served as Smarty's personal bodyguard. There was round the clock security which was provided by Philadelphia Park, but from January 8, 2004, the day Smarty Jones arrived in Hot Springs, Arkansas, until June 5, 2004, the day of the Belmont Stakes, Smarty and Bill were roomies.

Bill was bigger; Smarty ate more, Bill snores louder (according to Smarty, anyway)...and apparently Smarty wanted his MTV, while Bill is much more the country music maven. It didn't matter. The two men worked through their differences, and came out of the ordeal as still the best of friends.

Talk about "unbelievable," I wrote that line and read it over at least a dozen times before I realized that "I" had just referred to Smarty in a way that had attached some very humanistic qualities to "Mr. Smarty Jones."

I changed the line at least half as many times, before finally deciding that I was right the first time. Even if Smarty IS a horse, he was and is still a true friend to Bill Foster, and somehow I don't think either would be offended by the characterization.

Even though John was not bothered by the break neck pace that his personal schedule had taken on, or by the fact that unannounced guests from as far away as Australia were showing up at the gate, his wife was noticing some changes in the way in which the family was conducting its' business, and she wasn't happy about it.

"Family dinners were very important to us. Each of us had something to do with the cooking, and that stopped," Sherry Servis said. "Before the Preakness, our son, Tyler was having a problem in school. We gave him time to bring a grade up, and he said he did...but it turned out he was actually doing worse. That's why he wasn't allowed to go to the Preakness."

Sherry has always been a dominant force in the maintenance of this family unit. It was she who decided that she would take over the scheduling function in connection with media events. She was also directly responsible for demanding and then arranging for the enhanced security at Philadelphia Park, and the procurement of Lance Morrell to travel with John wherever he would go, day or night. Now, she was circling the wagons around her family as any lioness would, and making sure that proper perspective and priorities remained the order of each and every day.

She didn't have to wait long to realize yet one more success in this regard. Tyler's grades came up right after the Preakness. "He wasn't resentful or mad about missing the Preakness," Sherry told me. "He knew he messed up. He was a little bummed about being sent to a Convent while we were in Maryland, though." Sherry remembers Tyler's Convent experience being described by him as, "double punishment."

"We couldn't let this get away from us," Sherry said. "There was a lot left to do. We didn't know why our lives had been taken off into this direction. We were just going with the flow knowing that there was some purpose behind it all. But, we needed to be the same people after it was over, as we had been before it began."

That should have been a much harder task during these three weeks, than ever before. Day after day, Smarty Jones was the #1 most requested search criteria on Google, Yahoo, AOL and most other major internet search engines. As the close of each day brought Smarty and the Team one day closer to potential immortality, an additional five pound bag of laudatory references regarding the Team was heaped upon the bag that still resonated from having recently been hurled in their direction. The number of cards and letters which were being delivered to, or on behalf of Smarty Jones at this time was already in excess of five thousand pieces per day.

How Smarty managed to stay as relaxed as he did, is still hard to imagine.

How Sherry and Pat Chapman were able to play dueling ringmasters over this nine ring circus and keep their respective families' eyes on the real prize, is truly a testament to the strength of their character, and their understanding of what was really important.

Once focus and priorities had been readjusted and re-established, it was back to the business of getting ready for the Belmont. Once again, things were a little different in the mind of Smarty's Trainer, as he prepared primarily himself, for what lay ahead.

This was the first of the three races where Smarty would be the out and out "can't lose" favorite. He was the betting favorite at Post Time in

Kentucky, but that was in large part due to the huge bet laid down on him by C.J. Cella in an attempt to cover the Centennial Bonus. He went off as the favorite in Maryland also, but even then, there were still a gaggle of racing writers and prognosticators who had yet to buy into the Smarty Game Plan.

After he simply destroyed the entire field at the Preakness; and the WAY he did it, few if any suggested that Smarty wasn't already racing's twelfth ever Triple Crown Champion, weeks in advance of the final race taking place.

"The one thing a horseman HATES to hear," John bemoaned, "is that he CAN'T lose." "Early on, you know, when it was...win this one for Philadelphia; and later when it was win it for Pennsylvania, that's one thing...but when you got the WHOLE WORLD thinking, we FINALLY got a Triple Crown Winner...AND HE CAN'T LOSE...Man, THAT'S PRESSURE!"

For the most part, Smarty's Preakness victory had made believers out of almost all of the horse's former critics. Washington Post Racing Writer and respected thoroughbred expert, Andrew Beyer wrote, "The skeptics are silenced. Informed fans are convinced. Rival trainers are agog. All can jump on the Smarty Jones Bandwagon, now." Beyer, architect of the industry-respected "Beyer Speed Rating" and who prior to this time did NOT have a reserved seat on the previously-mentioned Smarty Jones Bandwagon, called Smarty's Preakness win, "one of the most convincing performances by a three year old in years."

Beyer himself had rewarded Smarty with the second highest Beyer Speed Rating in a Triple Crown Race, since 1987. However, while he seemed to suggest that Smarty would be racing's twelfth winner of the coveted Triple Crown, even at this late date in the game, Beyer seemed to be unable to resist taking one last minute shot at Smarty's heritage, noting that the horse was "not constituted to be an effective mile and a half runner."

A week ago, John might have read that part of the article and wondered WHAT Smarty Jones would have to do to convince some people. Today, he was so happy to see ANYONE not handing the race over to Smarty before it was run, that the knock on his horse didn't matter.

It didn't help that during the entire three week period, and while the Team was just trying to get themselves ready to race; one crazy offer after another was being thrust upon them. Jay Leno wanted to bring the horse to California and interview Smarty on "The Tonight Show." The White House Press Secretary's Office had called and extended an invitation to bring Smarty to the Rose Garden for a photo opportunity with the President. John took a phone call in his office early on in the week after the Preakness, from a guy who was getting married in a week and said he was willing to pay "any price" to have Smarty Jones pull his wedding carriage. Representatives of the movie production company Dreamworks were contacting

Philadelphia Park and asking to be put in touch with the Chapmans to discuss movie deals.

John may not have known at the time, and may not even know until he reads now but, before Smarty had even made it back to Philly Park after the Preakness, Bill Nack, who had written the authorized biography of the great Secretariat, was hired by Time Magazine to do the Cover Story for Time, which had already been given the title, "Born to Run," and would hit the streets according to one source, "the week after Smarty wins the Triple Crown."

John had treated Smarty's fans to a public gallop in advance of the Preakness, and now, on the verge of becoming the first Triple Crown Winner in nearly three decades, Smarty's Army wanted more. John didn't disappoint the fans, and neither did Smarty Jones. In his Post-Kentucky Derby public gallop, Smarty was greeted by somewhere between three thousand and five thousand fans, depending on whose estimate you were willing to accept. At his first Post-Preakness romp, no one put the numbers under five thousand. Fans started lining up at 5:30 am, and were ten deep at the rail before Smarty was anywhere in sight. "The noise was unlike anything that you would hear even on a regular race day," one Philly Park employee noted. John was more surprised, even than before. Smarty was even a little taken aback by the experience this time, too. "When he heard the crowd, he spooked just a little bit," John said. "We had to be careful about that. I didn't want him thinking that he was in a race and trying to open up."

If there was even a hint of remaining doubt as to what this experience was all about, all you had to do was look at the rail on the morning of this first Post-Preakness gallop. Not only were people ten deep at the rail, but the grandstand was full and there were people it seemed everywhere. At the rail itself, there was the kind of cooperation that you would quite clearly not expect to find in the city that not only booed Santa Clause, but also once threw the Dallas Cowboy Mascot out of the Upper Deck at Veteran's Stadium.

Today, despite the size of the crowd, and the desire on each fan's part to make sure that they got the best possible angle for their view of Smarty Jones; it was almost as though an unwritten code had been adopted. Big folks let the smaller folks get right up on the rail and then got in behind them. Dads who had kids on the shoulders got behind them. If you wanted to get even higher up, there were benches to stand on, farther back.

There were NO reported incidents of ANY KIND, no arrests, no infractions; just five thousand or more people, in a reasonably confined space, waiting for Smarty to make his appearance. The Track Announcer gave a proper introduction, Smarty galloped on by the grandstand, twice...and in a matter of literally minutes, once again, it was over.

People had spent two, three, four hours in

line, and in fifteen minutes, they were on there way back to their cars...and no one felt the least bit cheated.

Quite to the contrary, and down to the last fan, as a group those in attendance acted as though they had all just been Knighted by Queen Elizabeth II. As I walked out of the track that morning, people were just saying the same thing over and over, to whoever happened to be walking next to them at the time. "Did you see him. Did you see him?" "WOW...he was beautiful." "Isn't he amazing?"

At times the speaker was a child, talking to another child. Other times the words came from an adult, to another adult. The utterances that touched me deeply however, were those where it was not an overly excited child bubbling while babbling in the direction of an adult; but the little kid trapped in a mom or dad's body, who simply couldn't contain their own bounding joy as they addressed a child.

Thoroughbred racing has had great names in the last twenty-seven years. It has also had its' fair share of interesting stories to attach to those names. However, NOTHING had or has attracted the Youth of America to this industry.

On any regular racing day, at any track in the country...take a real good look at the people hanging over the rail and in the betting lines. You don't find many three, six or even nine year olds up on dad's shoulders.

Sure, many race tracks have taken to conducting "family days," even Philadelphia Park has them...and a special picnic area, just to accommodate the ten or twenty families who regularly attend the track on those days.

Today, more kids stood in line for a longer period time to watch a horse that wasn't even IN a race, than had come to the collection of North American Racetracks in an entire year, to actually participate in "family events."

Smarty Jones wasn't just "good for racing." He had already changed the look and feel of the spectator aspect of the sport, forever.

By this time, in late May 2004, Smarty Jones, John Servis and the Chapmans had received hundreds of thousands of pieces of mail. An astronomical number of these letters were simply addressed to "Smarty Jones, Philadelphia Park."

Ironic, is it not? The average person needs a nine digit zip code, a bar code, the proper Box Number or EXACT street address, or you end up paying a late charge on your mortgage payment because it didn't get to your lender on time.

When it came to finding Smarty Jones; even mail from overseas that was addressed ONLY to "Smarty Jones, USA" managed to find its' way to Barn 11 at Philadelphia Park.

A significant portion of the letters all began the same way. "Dear Smarty, I am sixty-three years old and have never written a fan letter to anyone in my entire life, but I am compelled to write to you." Well...the letters weren't ALL from people who were sixty-three, but if you left a blank where a person could have filled in their appropriate age, you might have sworn that many of the letters were form letters.

The letters came written in crayon, by children. They came written in crayon, BY ADULTS, who wanted to make sure that Smarty got the true flavor of what it was that their child had wanted to say to the horse, or to the trainer or owners. The letters came from each and every one of the fifty states, Washington, DC, Puerto Rico, and ultimately from thirty-five countries from around the world.

In some cases, one family member wrote on behalf of the entire family. In other cases, teachers wrote on behalf of entire classes of students. At other times, the letter was a large manila envelope containing individual letters written by each member of the class.

Even before the Belmont Stakes, Smarty Jones had been adopted by some fifty schools; not only in Philadelphia and the surrounding area, but also from New York, New Jersey, Ohio, Illinois, Florida, Kentucky and of course, Arkansas.

The collection of trinkets, booklets, scrapbooks, homemade ribbons and bows, horseshoe cutouts, and other items which were sent by the fans cluttered John's office, his home, the Chapmans' home, and any other area in which they were being housed.

One little girl sent Starlite Mints for Smarty, because her own horse "just loved them." Masters of desktop publishing, of all ages, created certificates of achievement in ALL forms, and sent them off to, "Smarty Jones, Philadelphia Park."

The letters told stories of inspiration and how Smarty overcoming his own injuries and other limitations gave both children and adults from around the world, the will not just to go on, but to win, at whatever particular challenge that writer faced. Those letters which didn't include some item which the writer wanted Smarty to have, requested something from Smarty, to give that writer something of Smarty's to allow them to use to build a bridge between the two. There were also the letters which reasonable, rational, logical adults wrote to Smarty Jones IN THE VOICE OF THEIR PETS, or in their own voice, and of course, the marriage proposals...most of which were written by those slightly less than rational adults, in their OWN voice.

Again, what struck me most about the mail at least at this particular point in time, was the fact that John and his wife, and Pat Chapman WERE RESPONDING to the letters; as many as possible ...while they were trying to train, prepare, and otherwise maintain a twenty-SEVEN hour a day schedule. "The letters were just amazing," Sherry Servis sighed. "I cried every time I sat down to read another one. These people were just wonderful, with the things they were saying about John and the Chapmans, and the way Smarty had somehow made their life better. I couldn't stop crying. We HAD to answer their letters."

In the meantime, there was yet another public

workout scheduled for Smarty Jones. This time, the gates opened even earlier in an effort to make it easier on the crowd, and to take into account the fact there might even be more people showing up, than for the previous gallop. More people did show up, too...MANY more. This time estimates on the low end were "WELL OVER TEN THOUSAND people," with one such estimate as high as EIGHTEEN THOUSAND, again, just to see the horse's morning jog.

Seeing an opportunity to make the experience a bit more entertaining for the fans, the Track Announcer had planned to turn things up a tad...really get everybody into it. This was, however, just the opposite of what John wanted to see happen, so before he got Smarty ready to hit the track, John sent someone to the Track Announcer's booth and asked him to tell the crowd to please not applaud or cheer while Smarty was actually working out, because John did not want Smarty to get too excited.

John and the others on the backside could actually hear the Track Announcer going through this explanation to the crowd, over the public address system.

"As we approached the track," John said, "you could hear a light roar." When John and Smarty got to the head of the stretch, they heard the Track Announcer say, "...If you look down to the head of the stretch...here comes Butterscotch and Smarty Jones."

"We got to the beginning of the grandstand," John said, "and it was dead silence." It was SO quiet that Pete looked over at John and said, "Oh my God, this is almost scary." Wearing a present day look of astonishment, John said, "You honestly could have heard a pin drop." His look then changing to one which included first a smile and then outright laughter, John continued, "It was like they were all saying to each other...shhhhhh, we gotta be quiet."

After John and Smarty were finished the workout, "they went BANANAS," John said. "They just went nuts. They were calling out to us as we jogged by. They were calling out directly to Smarty. And they kept saying thank you...thank you, not to ME," he laughed; "to the HORSE." "It was nothing like what we expected," Pete said. John agreed.

There was a lot going on away from the track during the Pre-Belmont period, as well. Among other things, the International Rating Agency, "Globeform," rated Smarty Jones the best horse to race anywhere in the world, giving Smarty a rating of 141, the highest rating issued to any horse since the organization began rating horses, in 1990.

Hollywood Park, in Los Angeles, California announced a promotion which it would conduct on the day of the Belmont Stakes, where the first ten thousand fans entering Hollywood Park would be given a $2.00 win ticket on Smarty Jones. Fans could either cash the ticket, in the event that Smarty won the race, or keep the ticket as a souvenir.

"Smarty Jones for President" bumper stickers began popping up; first in Kentucky, then later in Arkansas, Pennsylvania, and ultimately, New York, as well.

One Kentucky newspaper reported that their own Google search on Smarty Jones returned over 237,000 web page hits. Smarty's web hits on that day totaled more than the combined totals for NBA star Shaquille O'Neal, University of Kentucky basketball coach Rick Pitino, and 2003 Derby and Preakness Winner, Funny Cide, altogether, according to the newspaper.

As in the case of transporting Smarty Jones to Kentucky and Maryland, John was in no great hurry to leave the friendly and familiar confines of Philadelphia Park in favor of taking up temporary residence at Belmont.

Even though Smarty would be on his way to the Belmont Barn which had housed Secretariat during his pursuit of the Triple Crown, John would much rather see Smarty in surroundings which he knew, and which in John's mind at least, would provide Smarty with the highest possible comfort level.

Again, there was weeping and wailing and the occasional gnashing of teeth associated with John's decision. After all, Smarty was the Man/Horse of the hour. He had become a full-fledged, four alarm hero, and for as many as were able to see him at either of his public workouts in Philadelphia, or reporters who could report on him from Philly

Park; the vast majority of the press had already relocated to Belmont and more than a little bit anxiously awaited his arrival.

Officials at Belmont were pressing to get Smarty to New York as soon as possible also, if for no other reason than to stop having to share "their" press opportunities with Philadelphia Park. John wanted to cooperate with as many people as possible. He wanted to, and did continue to make himself available for press conferences, every day. He did early morning interviews with those who wanted or needed them. He met others at the Barn, at night, spoke at more school assemblies...he simply could not have been more cooperative. He just didn't really have a desire to get to Belmont until he absolutely had to do so. John also continued to keep Smarty on a very relaxed training schedule, enduring somewhat less criticism for the practice, in light of Smarty's record-setting win in the Preakness.

The time would come, however, when the trip to New York could be put off no longer. That day was June 2, 2004.

Every writer has tendencies or patterns which are part and parcel of their writing style, and which aid in the establishment of the writer's flavor, or flair. I didn't realize that I had any specific patterns, or groups of words that I tend to utilize maybe a little more than I should, until in the first draft of this work I noticed how many times I had written, "...one of the most amazing things..." and noted the number of things I had used the phrase in order to then describe. Had the subject of this work been anything OTHER THAN Smarty Jones, and his personal transformation from a participant in multiple near-death experiences, to underdog or sentimental favorite racehorse, to Kentucky Derby Winner, to sports hero...to hero...to worldwide cultural icon; perhaps I would be more concerned. You couldn't accurately write this story and NOT refer to one "amazing thing" after another, because that IS the story, in and of itself.

Having said that, "one of the most amazing things" which occurred not just at this moment in the storyline, but during the entire Smarty Saga, was Smarty's trip from Philadelphia Park to Belmont.

If you think in terms of that transformation which I previously mentioned; Smarty's "arrivals" at various locations along this journey were perhaps the one event which told you exactly what the racing world, and later the entire world was thinking about the horse at those specific moments in time.

When Smarty Jones arrived in Hot Springs, on January 8, 2004, the only people who even knew he was coming were the people who were in the same van with him. To the guard at the back gate, this particular van was just another in a long line of vans which would find their way into and out of the Oaklawn Jockey Club over the next three months, and might just as well have been transporting a horse named "Fred Smith," as opposed to "Smarty

Jones."

When Smarty finally got to Churchill Downs, after his one week diversion to Keeneland, he was still one of more than the maximum allotted number of twenty Derby hopefuls; and even though his position in the field was secured by virtue of his having won the Arkansas Derby, his arrival was "without fanfare." No one went out of there way to find out what time Smarty was leaving Keeneland, or when he would be arriving at Churchill. The few racing writers who happened to be in the area when Smarty bounded off the van at Churchill Downs for the first time gave a wink and a nod to John, snapped a photo or two, if that, and moved on.

After the Derby win, but still not having convinced the press corps of his worthiness to star status, Smarty's arrival at Pimlico was, while "much anticipated," still not going to have many of racing's media elite moving their spa appointments back in order to make sure they were able to personally cover the event.

Three week's later, the vast majority of these same journalists would have postponed their own heart transplant, not only to add their personal commentary to his "arrival" at Belmont, but also to his "DEPARTURE" from Philadelphia Park.

Smarty Jones exodus from Bensalem, Pennsylvania, on the morning of June 2, 2004 will universally go down in history as one of, if not THE all-time greatest transportation event associated with ANY sport. Not even the Baltimore Colts midnight move to Indianapolis decades ago, will be remembered any longer as the most noteworthy sports transportation benchmark.

Team Smarty had arrived early this morning. John wanted to let Smarty run before making the drive to New York. Though for security reasons not all of the specific details of Smarty's travel were made public in advance, by 9:30 AM, when it was time to load Smarty Jones into the van, it was as if an infomercial had run on ESPN for the entire week previous, just to make sure everybody knew the exact moment the trip would begin and the route to be taken.

There was little chance that THIS arrival would be "without fanfare." Hell, the DEPARTURE had more fanfare than the announcement of the verdict at the OJ Trial. In terms of Smarty's pending arrival at Belmont, perhaps we can all agree that the phrase "much anticipated" just wouldn't do proper justice to the thought process of those already in attendance on the backside of that racetrack, either.

Before Smarty even made it to the van that morning, he was greeted by in excess of five hundred reporters, photographers, cameramen and women, as well as other various and especially sundry individuals. No offense intended by the "sundry" remark, after all...it was about 5:00 in the morning when many of the crews started to show up.

Now, after a morning workout and a quick bath for the object of all of this attention, it was time to load up. In what had come to be not only typical Smarty Jones fashion, but something absolutely expected of him by the media who by now had come to know him so very well; Smarty moseyed out of his stall, casually made his way to where the shutters were clicking and then stopped, just long enough to nonverbally inquire as to whether the crowd had gotten all that they needed, so he could get down to the business of business... and then trotted into his Hilton on Wheels.

Local police cars, sirens blaring and lights flashing, took up residence to Smarty's front and rear. As impressive as all of this was already, it was still a very controlled environment, attended exclusively by people who either had to be there because it was their job, or wanted very much to be there because they were in some way affiliated with the racetrack, the horse, or someone else who was required to be up at that hour. It wouldn't take long however, to see just how important this trip was to the average man, woman, or child on the street.

With more helicopters than you would see covering a fifty car pileup on any major highway in this country, Smarty's heavily guarded mobile palace made its' way down the backside drive and headed toward the exit. The lead police escort had-n't even set a front tire onto a city street, when everyone knew just how different this trip was going to be. Notwithstanding the best efforts of the local police, track security and others, fans had parked their cars farther up and down the road, away from the Park Gates, and then walked to get to as close to the gate area as they could and just stood on the side of the road waving and cheering.

As the caravan made it onto the city streets and entered the few residential neighborhoods that would have to be traversed on the way to the entrance to the Pennsylvania Turnpike, moms and dads, grandparents, kids who stayed home from school, and any one else who heard the sirens, waved and wished well from their front lawns, or hanging out of doors or windows. Traffic just stopped on its' own. Horns honked...it was no different than the response any professional sports team receives AFTER they win a championship.

When Smarty and his escorts made it to the entrance to the Pennsylvania Turnpike, all toll collection ceased in both directions, so that the toll takers could all exit their toll booths and come out to wish their best to Smarty Jones.

Just down the road a few miles, where the Pennsylvania Turnpike meets up with the New Jersey Turnpike at the State Line, the same scene played out with Smarty receiving an outlaying of best wishes from employees of the Garden State, as the escort function was transferred from local and state police from Pennsylvania, to the New Jersey State Police.

Two of the officers from the Pennsylvania side, Officers Gladu and Hanrahan, told one reporter following the van that they had been on a security detail assigned to President George W. Bush not less than six months prior to this time, and that the President of the United States did not receive anything close" to the response that the crowd afforded to Smarty Jones.

Just over an hour later, The New Jersey Authorities passed Smarty off to New York State Troopers, and about a half hour after that, local television and radio stations broke into regular programming with an announcement that Smarty Jones had arrived at Belmont Park.

Team Smarty had made it to New York. While the good people at Belmont would have loved to have had Smarty make his first appearance a few weeks earlier in order to have shared in the larger portion of the pre-race period of Smarty Mania, track officials were poised to receive an overflow crowd and record wagering on the big race.

More than one thousand employees would be on hand at the track on race day to handle crowd control and to receive and process wagers. The Chairman of the New York Racing Association in welcoming the horse would make reference to Smarty Jones as "the biggest box office draw in New York" in quite some time.

For John and the 170 members of the group that was now traveling with him, the last two days before the race would be the most difficult. He still hated the fact that the only comment he was hearing form anyone was that Smarty couldn't lose.

Some of the same local and national writers who had only five weeks ago called into question whether Smarty should have been ALLOWED to race in the Derby were now penning columns where they openly declared that the only issue remaining to be decided at the Belmont Stakes was "how much" Smarty would win by, and would he break Secretariat's record for margin of victory.

"The pressure from the media in those last two days was pretty intense," John recalled, "but other than falling asleep and missing a scheduled interview with Mike and the Mad Dog...it went about as smooth as it could." "I guess Mike and the Mad Dog were pretty upset," John chuckled, "but...man, I had been going nonstop for months, and I just passed out." Mike Francesa and Chris "the Mad Dog" Russo host a popular New York City Sports Talk Show on radio station WFAN during the afternoon drive portion of the day.

John was scheduled to appear the day after he and Smarty arrived in New York. Smarty's arrival was BIG NEWS in the City, and every sports talk show host wanted to draw first blood among their colleagues, by landing John before anyone else. As usual, John was happy to oblige. On this day however, John rose at his customary early hour, went to the track, waded through the hoard of media who were now equally adept at making a 5 AM arrival...and worked his horse.

Following the workout there was the customary morning press conference, followed by a series of not less than fifteen interviews which had been requested by news agencies including ESPN, CNN, and the BBC, with of course, his every move being chronicled by a Japanese camera crew which was producing a documentary on the story of the great racehorse. All of this was followed by a Press Luncheon, another Press Briefing, the day's final photo opportunity...leaving John about ninety minutes to shower, change and make it to his scheduled appearance on the afternoon radio program. "I got back to the hotel, got in the shower, and thought...I have got to lay down for about thirty minutes. No problem though, I can still make it, easy."

Several hours later...John realized that things often DO get to a point where the body simply takes over. "I felt bad for Mike, and of course the Mad Dog," John said. "They seemed like pretty nice guys, but they were seriously upset about the whole thing."

If he had time, I am more than certain that John would have made it up to the two disgruntled radio talk show hosts, but...each and every day, there were more and more events, and exactly the same number of hours within which to accomplish them.

And, while John would never come out and say this...because it just isn't in him to say it; my advice to Mike and the Mad Dog is to rest assured that this will not be their last opportunity to interview John Servis on his way to winning a Triple

Crown. Keep smiling and don't be TOO upset, and my guess is that you will be at the head of the class, once again, when it comes to getting the first shot at bringing this great trainer to your listeners.

As more of "the Gang of 170" began to arrive in New York, John was reunited with his friends Brent and Zach, who came in from Hot Springs, Arkansas for the race. Brent and Zach are two guys in their late-20's who John had met through Jockey Willie Martinez, while Smarty was training and racing in Arkansas. Both are in the general vicinity of 6'4" and collectively tip the scales at just under 500 pounds of human being.

"Hey, they seemed like good guys, and I didn't know anybody in Arkansas when I first got there," John laughed, "so we started hanging out." One night John and "the boys" went to hit baseballs at a field. They went out to dinner together pretty regularly, and then later, Brent and Zach started showing up at the track in the mornings to watch Smarty train. "They kinda became my groupies," John said with a grin.

John had arranged for Brent and Zach to come to the Derby and Preakness, and now they were even being written about in local Arkansas papers, referred to only as "The Followers of Smarty Jones." In the period between the Preakness and Belmont Stakes, reporters started to ask John about Brent and Zach. Thinking he would have a little fun with anyone so starved for yet ADDITIONAL Smarty Jones information so as to need to know all there was to know about his friends, John decided to tell people that Brent and Zach were his bodyguards.

On Wednesday afternoon, June 2nd, after John had finished attending the pre-race draw for position, John met up with Brent and Zach in the lobby of the Garden City Hotel to wait for Stewart Elliott to arrive. Stew had just arrived after having a mount in a race at Monmouth Park earlier that afternoon. Stew was apparently very tired, but was immediately surrounded and swarmed upon the moment he entered the lobby of the hotel. Witnessing the scene with John as they stood across the room in the Lobby bar, one of the Arkansas guys looks up, "just like he really was a bodyguard," John roared, "and says, C'MON...Stew needs our help!"

"These guys go flying through the lobby as though they were parting the Red Sea along the way. They grab Stew, get him checked in, and then walk on either side of him to escort him to his room." By the time Brent and Zach returned to the lobby, it was now John who had a crowd around him. When the guys reached John, one of them announced, "We put him to bed, Boss. Everything's good."

"From that moment on," John said, "everyone really believed they were my bodyguards." Major news outlets started asking John for interview time and opportunities...with his bodyguards.

It wasn't only John doing his best to keep the

mood as light as possible in the final forty-eight hours before the biggest race in history. Sherry did her part in this regard, also...even if unintentional.

John was at the barn with Smarty on Friday, while Sherry was back at the Garden City Hotel. Sherry needed to get to the barn, but since John had their personal VISAmobile with him, she would need to get a ride to the track from someone else. This shouldn't be a problem, since there were still 168 other people in their group, many of whom had vehicles of their own which were there and available for use.

In the lobby of the hotel, Sherry ran into their friend "Louie," who was literally just returning to the hotel. Sherry told Louie of her plight and, being the gentleman that he is, Louie told Sherry that his truck was "right out front and still running" since he had been waiting to have the car parked. Sherry thanked her friend, ran out the front door, jumped in the truck and was off to the track.

At the barn, mind you, there are barricades set up everywhere, so as to limit the ability of maneuver in the backside area. In this particular case, you really couldn't get any closer to Smarty's temporary living space than the inside rail area.

Sherry had been at the barn now for about two hours, when a very large group of reporters began to congregate in the area outside of the barn in anticipation of John addressing them at some point. As Sherry stood by the barn herself, in advance of this impromptu press event, there was a man standing in, oh...about the middle of the gaggle of media types, who himself... was clearly NOT a card carrying member of ANY journalistic organization. In fact, the "card" this gentlemen was, or was not carrying, perhaps, is still open to question. In any event, this particular individual is JUMPING up and down waving his arms and quite clearly trying to get "someone's" attention prior to the onset of any festivities.

At this point, Sherry turns to John and tells him, "That guy jumping up and down...he looks like the valet guy...from the hotel." Being the concerned citizen she is, generally, Sherry made her way through the crowd of reporters to make contact with the obviously distressed young man. Being the problem solver that we know her to be, Sherry was certain in her own mind that she could take care of whatever it was which might be distressing him.

"You...took the truck," the out of breath little man attempted to bark out over and over again in a way which made it clear that English wasn't even his SECOND language. Sherry's response, once she had any idea at all of what was being said to her was, "What?"

"You took the man's truck," our "Guest Worker" professed, yet again. "Yes," Sherry replied, finally able to glean the specific thought that was attempting to be conveyed. "I took the man's truck."

"He...he, was trying to check out," was the reply.

Alright, so...as in the case of her husband, John, at Pimlico, when he was relating his OWN truck story...this SHOULD have been a time when the story itself moved directly from the "here's what happened phase" to the "it's like this...I took the wrong truck, everybody goes home, happy ending phase." But noooooooooooo, haha. Pulling a lesson RIGHT out of her husband's playbook, Sherry immediately needed me to know that, "it was the same color, and everything."

Remember, Sherry had been at the barn, by this time, for over two hours before "Valet Man" had even found her. Apparently, the truck she took had belonged to a gentlemen who was in fact, attempting to check out, and had directed the valet to bring his car around. Yes, in fact, as Louie had suggested, his truck WAS at valet, running, and waiting to be parked. Further in fact, TWO HOURS LATER, Louie's truck was STILL at valet...RUNNING...and waiting to be parked, while Sherry had jumped in THE OTHER truck that was also "running" and took off.

(Note to self...never let EITHER of the Servises borrow my truck. Apparently they have "issues." Haha.)

The whole experience was however, just what the doctor ordered. It got everybody's mind off of how intense those last few days and weeks had become.

Pat and Chappy were totally committed to media avoidance at this point. They had been getting hounded, and what with Chappy still not being in the best of health, the kind of press ringer that they were being put through was just too much to deal with at that moment. They were still receiving bags, and bags, and bags of mail everyday, at EACH of their two homes, and responding to well into the hundreds of requests that they appear here, there and everywhere to either accept an award, christen a sloop, dedicate a coffee shop, or preside over the birth of kittens, among other things.

Pat did find herself in the subject line of yet another one of this story's most humorous anecdotes during the Post-Preakness period, however. After her horse had already won the first two legs of the VISA Triple Crown, and while grocery shopping in a local supermarket near their home just outside of New Hope, Pennsylvania, Pat had her own VISA card declined. She remembers the young clerk at the store being even more embarrassed than she was over the incident. "You can't be declined," she told her. "Let's keep trying." Apparently there were some charges which Pat didn't know about, perhaps relating to the damage to an ignition locking system on an SUV that was used by John Servis several weeks earlier? Everything was straightened out, though...Pat made it home with the coffee and VISA will from now on be known as "the card that is accepted everywhere ...unless you're the owner of a horse who is about to actually WIN the VISA Triple Crown Bonus."

John and Sherry meanwhile, remained the

flash point of the daily firestorm, and though they worked very hard never to allow the world to see them sweat, it was pretty clear by this time that win or lose, they would just rather that the ordeal be over.

Nome, Alaska was starting to look pretty good to the Servis Family these days, too. Win or Lose.

CHAPTER TWELVE

THE NOT SO BEST OF TIMES

From before even the birth of this remarkable racehorse, we were able to realize now in
hindsight that not only did one thing after another,
after another, after another have to go "just right"
in order for him to enjoy any life successes; but that
it did, it did, and it did do so, yet again. Whenever
Smarty Jones needed a miracle; whenever he needed to be touched by the hand of the Fates, the
Racing Gods, The Grand High Determiner of All
Things, or whatever other Supreme Entity that you
recognize...he was so touched, as were the people
around him.

Six times in the last eight racing seasons, a thoroughbred racehorse would make its' way to the Belmont Stakes positioned to become only the twelfth in history to leave the famed raceway wearing each and every one of the trappings associated with having earned the title of Triple Crown Champion. In not one of the previous racing seasons, were so many, so certain, that "this is the year."

Hall of Fame Jockey Steve Cauthen, who was aboard Affirmed when racing's last Triple Crown was captured in 1978, broke his silence on this year's Candidate by saying, "It's time for the coronation of a new Champion. It's what racing needs, and what everyone is waiting for." And, With only hours to go, it looked as though the Fates, and those other Supernatural Entities had clearly taken whatever steps would be required in order to further solidify the immortal position of this sport's newest superstar.

But, this wasn't just another horse. This was Smarty Jones. This was a being who began his life as a "four year old boy trapped in a horse's body," and who, in three short years, had become a forty year old, still encased in the same equine shell. One writer for The Bloodhorse Magazine suggested after observing Smarty Jones throughout the entire Triple Crown experience; "This horse knows more about the BUSINESS of racing than many of the humans who are actually making decisions." He would have to make a decision or two this day, to keep his string of victories intact.

The day got off to a fine start. Rather remarkably, all of the members of the Team got a pretty good night's sleep. The only minor glitch in the early going was that Sherry Servis left the hotel wearing something other than her "lucky black and white" colors, which she had worn for all of Smarty's other races. She had plenty of time to get back to the hotel and change, however, so...no harm, no foul.

The officials at Belmont Park were more than pleased to see that their earlier predictions regarding crowd size and the amount of money projected to be wagered on the race were, while definitely record breaking, were not even close to the actual totals in either category. There were actually MORE people than they had anticipated; and the people wagered even MORE than had been projected.

A total of 120,139 fans poured into the facility, TRASHING the previous attendance record by more than 17,000. Wagering was just under $111,000,000.00, or roughly $13,000,000.00 higher than any previous Belmont Stakes Race.

There was a weather front coming in, which projected to blanket the area in and around Elmont, New York, with moderate to heavy rains at, or about the time which was set for the race to begin. While no one associated with Team Smarty bought into the writer's earlier theory that Smarty's Kentucky Derby victory was at all based upon the fact that it had been run "in slop," it was clear that

Smarty didn't mind making the trip on a wet surface. It was equally clear that some of the same horses who didn't fare as well at the Derby weren't quite as comfortable playing in the rain, as Smarty. In that sense, the weather report was just one more indication that today would be, all that it had been billed as, for the previous three weeks.

Regardless of what anyone had ever written, said or even thought about Smarty Jones, positive or negative, there was one astounding quality which had dominated not only his racing career, but his entire life. In a sea of inconsistency; he was consistently consistent. New trainer after yours is murdered; no problem. Smash your head on an iron bar and almost end your own life; no problem. Face setback after setback, win race after race and have some experts still bad mouth you; no problem.

John Servis said it best when he said very early on in the process, "All this horse does, is win...at some point that fact will have to be acknowledged."

As it came to within moments of the start of the Belmont Stakes, if there were any experts left who had not already pledged allegiance to Smarty Jones, they were standing with their hand over their heart just waiting for him to cross the finish line, in order that they might do just that.

So many times in life however, we tend to be able to get our hands around "the Brass Ring," but for some reason, acquisition of the prize ultimately eludes our grasp.

For readers under the age of forty, there was a time when every carousel, or merry-go-round in this great nation had a machine that was attached to it. The machine had an arm which extended into the carousel itself. At some time, close to the end of each ride, the arm would swing around, so that if you were hanging off of the side of the carousel, or at least standing close to the edge, you could reach out and attempt to grab one of the brass rings that the machine offered. Being able to master the fine art of "grabbing the brass ring" was something not only to be proud of, but was also something of a badge of honor within families, and among friends.

I'm not sure if the brass rings are all gone now because they were all stolen; or because lawyers finally got around to suing carousel operators when kids like me fell off of the ride while trying to actually grab the brass ring...or, if that is just a slice of Americana that went the way of the five cent cigar, penny candy, and dew in the afternoon; but since the reference is more than appropriate here, I felt an explanation was in order.

Usually, when we get to that point where you can start to see the wheels coming off of your OWN personal success story, it is something that YOU see at least a little bit before those around you. Then, you choose; elect to just ignore the telltale indicia of disaster and continue to press forward, or cheerlead to those around you while internally you realize that the beginning of the end is at hand.

Smarty never saw the wheels come off in this

instance. He never knew the beginning of the end was at hand, until he had been passed for the very first time in his illustrious racing career. Smarty was being himself; consistently consistent...running the race that he knew he was going to run, the way in which he knew he would run it.

John saw it coming though, and much earlier than he would have liked to have witness that fact.

John's recounting of each of Smarty's earlier races was, as previously mentioned, one of the highlights of my research in connection with this book. Personally, I have more respect for John Servis than I have conveyed in any conversation I have had with this man. The passion which he holds, not only for the sport of thoroughbred racing, but for the people he works with, the animals he works with, his family, friends, and life in general, is not only personally rewarding to those who are for-tunate enough to make his acquaintance, but equal-ly beneficial to the entire community of human beings who call this planet, "home." It is because of this kind of passion and zest for life that we ALL win.

John's call of the Belmont Stakes, went some-thing like this...

"When they turned at the top of the back stretch and Bailey (aboard Eddington) got outside of Smarty, that bothered me. As soon as he did that, Smarty JUMPED into the bridle and wanted to go.

He needed to settle. The time was okay, and with Bailey and Solis (on Rock Hard Ten) running, they wouldn't be around at the end. When the first half mile had gone up in :48, I thought, Okay, okay, he can do this, no problem. Then the second half went up in :46, and I thought, OH NO! All I could hope for at that point was that there was nobody behind him."

The passion that I spoke of earlier was near overflowing now, as John relayed this story to me months after the event had taken place. As the television cameras went to close up on John during the event itself, he was rock solid, never wavering for a moment; the consummate professional.

Sitting alongside of him this day, I knew for the first time that he is not only a great trainer, but a great actor, as well. He was dying inside, THIS day; telling me what he thought and how he felt THAT day. I can't even begin to imagine what he was going through in the last half mile of the Belmont stakes.

"It was at this point that I started to scan the field," John sighed. "Birdstone was starting to make a run as Smarty Jones went farther into the lead. At the turn for home, Birdstone was really running. His strides were lengthening, while Smarty was starting to shorten his. I could see that Smarty was tired, and was just hoping that Birdstone would flatten out...but he didn't."

"When they turned for home," John said, "it was SO LOUD that in the racetrack, you couldn't hear the track announcer anymore." "Then, they got to seventy yards from the finish...and it was like the day of Smarty's last workout at Philly Park; you literally could hear a pin drop. It was DEAD SILENCE...and it stayed that way for what seemed like, ever."

After describing all of the other races Smarty had won, I asked John how he felt at the moment that he first realized that his horse was going to win. I didn't ask him how he felt when he realized Smarty would be passed by Birdstone. The look on his face more than adequately answered the question without that issue ever being addressed.

After an easily explainable, but very long pause, John kept our conversation going by adding, "It goes back to the thing about everybody thinking that there was no way the horse could lose," he said. "There's one way to win a race, and a thousand ways to lose."

Many people who were in Belmont Park on June 5, 2004, attempted to describe their impressions of the last ten seconds of the race, and how they perceived the crowd response. One told me, "It was like the entire racetrack had been sucked into a black hole. It wasn't just that you could have heard a pin drop. That place stayed COMPLETELY SILENT for several minutes." Another individual suggested that the period of silence was "at least thirty to forty-five seconds." And, yet a third person made it clear that the period of post-race silence was longer and even MORE silent that the formal "moment of silence" which had been requested before the race began, in memory of Former President Ronald Reagan, who had died earlier that same day.

When the silence was finally broken, not just at Belmont Park, but around the world...the tears began to flow. Toddlers to Senior Citizens everywhere felt a sense of loss unlike anything which could otherwise be rationally explained away.

At Smarty's home track, Philadelphia Park, over twenty thousand people had packed the facility in support of his effort. Not one of those twenty thousand fans could comprehend Smarty being passed at the finish line. In eight races Smarty had led each and every race when he entered the stretch run, and had never once even been passed by another horse once he made it to the stretch. "IT'S THE CURSE," one of the Philly Park faithful screamed out, referring to the long line of "almosts" in Philadelphia sports history. Others at the racetrack couldn't even bring themselves to speak. Sandra Ciprich, was one of the twenty thousand plus who came to Philadelphia Park to watch the Belmont Stakes. "Before the race, people were screaming and cheering," she said. "Everyone just KNEW Smarty was going to win. Afterward, it was quiet at first, but then people just started crying, and literally throwing themselves down on the ground. It was like somebody died."

Fans at Smarty's adopted home in Arkansas didn't fare much better, either. The Oaklawn Jockey

Club sported perhaps the largest Smarty Party this, or any side of Belmont Park. Nearly fifteen thousand more fans had filled Oaklawn this day. Here, the post-race silence would be broken not by the mention of any "curse"...but by the tear-filled voice of a lone woman who attempted to inform the world, "We...still love you, Smarty Jones..."

In a crowded sports bar in Orange County, California, one Smarty fan simply repeated, "he went out to soon...he went out too soon," over and over while wiping away tears of his own.

The silence in Pat and Chappy's box was finally broken by John, when he turned to Roy and said, very simply, "We got beat." Chappy wanted to know, "What happened? Did the Jockey move too soon?" "No," John said, "We just got beat."

John may have known that Smarty got beat, but Smarty didn't. He actually thought that he had won, and after the race, he made a move on his own to get to the Winner's Circle. "He actually thought he had won the race," Sherry said. And, why shouldn't he think that way? He had ended up in the Winner's Circle in each and every one of his eight previous outings. Today, more than ANY other...it was where he was supposed to be. It was where the world wanted him to be. It was where so many had NEEDED him to be...and yet, as he pulled his rider toward victory lane, Stew was reluctantly able to muster the strength to nonverbally tell his partner, "no...not today, my friend."

NBC television cameras immediately went

close up on John as the two horses barreled across the finish line. His disappointment was evident, though it was his professionalism, class manner of responding and incredible character which struck not only the television commentators, but an entire world of distraught Smarty fans. Pat Chapman was most concerned about the impact the loss might have on her husband's health and wanted to get him to a safer and more secure location at the earliest possible opportunity. One microphone after another was being thrust at the group requesting, or even demanding their "reaction"...before any member even had a chance to decide how they really felt. Sherry Servis was as she had been so many times, for so many throughout the course of the entire experience, a veritable pillar of internal strength. "We all wanted to breakdown...right then and there," she said. "But, we had to keep it together, for the people, and for Smarty. The kids were in tears, but the whole world was watching, and we needed to maintain our composure. Smarty Jones deserved to be remembered as being among that group of horses that would be remembered as the best of all-time. The world needed that, and that was the impression that we all needed to convey." Like I said...an absolutely amazing display of strength, when you consider that your heart, along with at least a part of your soul has just been ripped out.

John then went off to find Birdstone's Trainer, Nick Zito, and offer his best wishes and congratulations.

John didn't tell me this, but Nick Zito did. When John approached Zito after the race and offered congratulations on the victory, Zito was the first to apologize for having won the race. According to Nick, "John looked at me and said... don't apologize for anything, you ran a great race. Enjoy the victory." Like I said, how do you not have awe inspiring respect for John Servis? If there was ever a horse which truly deserved to complete the Triple Crown, it was Smarty Jones. Likewise, no Trainer in the history of this great trilogy was and is more deserving of the honor, than is John Servis.

Ironically, of all of the other "name Trainers" in the 2004 series of Triple Crown races, John and Nick "knew" each other much better than John knew any of the others. One of John's other owners had actually moved his horses out of John's barn at some point and given them over to Nick Zito for training. Apparently this happens from time to time in the horse business, but according to Nick, "Usually the guy who loses the horses will hate you for life. John wasn't that way. We stayed friends." Even more ironically, the same owner later pulled the horses from Zito's Barn and gave them back to John Servis. One of that owner's horses is now a leading prospect to compete in the 2005 Kentucky Derby. When I asked Zito how he felt about that, he just laughed and said, "I won't hate John for life, either."

After offering his congratulations to Nick Zito,

John went to talk to Stewart Elliott. By the time John reached the barn, Stew was already being "blamed" for the loss. Even today, there are a contingent of racing aficionados who continue to suggest that Stew simply "took the horse out, too fast." John wanted his rider to know that he had ridden a good race and that he had nothing to feel bad about. "Once they hooked him up and started pushing him, he couldn't get him to settle after that," John said. "There was nothing Stew could have done about that."

Almost immediately after the race, while Edgar Prado (Birdstone's Jockey) was also apologizing for winning, to anyone who he could find to talk to, controversy started to brew about a possible conspiracy on the part of Jerry Bailey (Eddington) and Alex Solis (Rock Hard Ten) and how the two allegedly sacrificed there own horses' chances at winning, just to make sure that Smarty (and perhaps more significantly, Stew) didn't win.

Publicly, no one has, nor likely ever will own up to anything in this respect. In writing about the actions of the two jockeys in Bloodhorse magazine, Steve Haskin suggested that he thought it, albeit perhaps "naively" so, highly unlikely that anyone in the racing industry would not want to see a Triple Crown Winner, given the enhanced popularity a thing like that would bring to the sport. Other writers were equally convinced that there were forces at work who simply did not want Smarty's name added to the list of Triple Crown Winners.

Haskin went further in his proffered explanation of events, to suggest that earlier in the week leading up to the race, one of the other exercise riders had been speaking to one of the two jockeys involved and flat out suggested that "the only way to beat Smarty Jones" was "to press him." There is no question that these two jockeys pressed him... and another horse won the race.

To the credit of John Servis, and the Chapmans, they have never once commented or taken a position on the outcome of the race, other than as John did in the box on race day, when he told his owner, "We just got beat."

As an admittedly somewhat less than objective observer of the post-race discussion of the events I can only note that neither Alex Solis, nor Jerry Bailey were aboard Rock Hard Ten, or Eddington when each horse came out of the gate in their respective races following the Belmont.

I do not say this so as to make the claim that there was any reason at all for either jockey change, other than the general unavailability of those riders at the time of the Haskell Invitational, in the case of Rock Hard Ten, or the Travers Stakes in the case of Eddington. I just note that the changes were made.

Meanwhile, back at Belmont Park, and in simulcasting facilities around the world; in restaurants, sports bars, private homes, airport terminals, bus stations, and in quite literally millions of locations all around the world, people wept openly...over the results of a horse race.

For the first and only time in his racing career, Smarty Jones was denied entry into the Winner's Circle. For the sixth time in eight years, the Belmont Stakes deprived the racing world a Triple Crown Winner. This time, however, the entire world was denied a coronation. Never before had so many who cared so little about racing, cared so much about the outcome of this one very special race.

In the three weeks between the Preakness and Belmont Stakes, racing insiders wrote over and over about "how ready racing was" to receive a new Triple Crown Champion. This may have been true. But if these same insiders had found there way outside, for even a moment, their story would have been, not even how prepared the world had made itself to receive Smarty Jones as its' universal rallying point...but how much we as a community of people NEEDED that to occur. And, before Birdstone even had his opportunity to smile for the cameras, it was clear that even his handlers were members of that same community.

The people who won the race, didn't believe that they could win before the race started...and didn't want the win, after it was over. Nick Zito apologized to John, privately. Edgar Prado, Birdstone's Jockey apologized on national television, while he was still on the horse, and before he had even made his way to the Winner's Circle. Mary Lou Whitney, and her husband John Hendrickson, owners of Birdstone called the Chapmans the following day and made a similar apology as well. Somehow I just don't see ANY owner, player or manager, in ANY other sport, EVER...apologizing for winning.

John Hendrickson told me, "This Triple Crown Series was a magic moment in all of sports history. If Mary Lou and I were excited about ANYTHING, It was simply to have been a part of it. We became Smarty Jones fans after the Preakness, and we still are, today." John went on to say that his horse was beaten in the Kentucky Derby by Smarty Jones, but felt no shame in "losing to a horse that was greatness personified." "We did NOT want to be spoilers, at ALL," John said. "We were in AWE of Smarty Jones, just like the rest of the entire world. Smarty is OUR hero, too...and better than ninety percent of what we are feeling now, and felt from the time that the race ended...is remorse."

I'm not sure Nick Zito wanted this fact known, but according to Zito, his instructions to Edgar Prado that day, which came direct from the horse's owners, were to "do your best to finish second."

Individuals who are of a competitive spirit will often tell you that "if winning didn't matter, they wouldn't keep score." I can safely say that there are few, if any more competitive souls on earth, than John Hendrickson. Yet the sincerity in his voice as he himself held back tears while speaking in such glowing terms about Smarty Jones and reiterating how saddened he and his wife were over their victory made the impact that this horse had on even the most competitive among us, even more apparent.

John Hendrickson did say that he was very happy for his Trainer to have won the Belmont. "It was a huge win for Nick, and we were very happy about that," he said, "but knowing that the entire rest of the world wanted the other horse to win... we've made more apologies in the last month then Senator Lott." (Referencing a situation involving the United States Senator who was forced to resign from a leadership position after ill-received comments made at a birthday cerebration for Senator Strom Thurmond.)

I asked John Hendrickson if there was one thing that he could say, about the race, and about Smarty Jones, to anyone who would listen;what would he say?

"We caught a break," he said. "What happened in that race does not change for an instant, what Smarty Jones meant to racing, or to the world. Smarty was every bit the hero after that race, as he was before, and every bit the racehorse, also. Our horse? A month from now we'll be the only people who even remember his name. Smarty Jones? He'll be remembered by a lot of people, for a long time."

Looks like you don't have to finish second to demonstrate what class is all about, after all.

There was however, at least one relationship casualty which was born out of the result of this race. Hall of Fame Trainer, Bobby Frankel, a long time friend of Nick Zito is alleged to have gone out of his way to tell Zito just exactly how lucky he really was to have won the Belmont Stakes with Birdstone. Reportedly, Frankel told Zito, "You could race against that horse (Smarty Jones) fifty times, and never beat him again." As sorry as Nick was to have actually won the race in the first place...it's quite another thing to have someone throw your good fortune in your face when you're already trying to be gracious.

By Zito's own admission, the two haven't exchanged so much as a "hi or goodbye" ever since.

Again, to the credit of the other A-List Trainers, but even moreso to the credit of John Servis...John was contacted by virtually every trainer except one after the Belmont, and not only congratulated by them all, but also essentially welcomed into "the club." "You'll be back," one of them said. "Just promise you won't beat me so bad on the next go round."

Months after the Belmont, as I asked Pat and Chappy to take me back to how they remember the end of the day, Pat broke down, as I did, during our conversation. "It really hasn't sunk in until today," she said. "...what it cost THE FANS..."

"You simply cant believe what it was like to be in that racetrack," Pat said. "As Smarty was coming down the stretch, there was this deafening electric roar that got louder, and louder and louder, until people finally realized that another horse was catching up, and then just like someone turned the

volume on a TV set completely off, there was quiet...
and then the quiet turned to dead silence." "Not
only did the silence go on, forever, but when you
think about it...the silence was actually louder in
some senses, than the roar."

As Pat and Chappy later left the racing facility, Pat had asked the press to give them some time,
and told them that Chappy was just not up to talking to anyone, about anything. The press, to its'
credit honored that request, and Smarty's Owners
made there way to the exit. At the time, it was little
consolation, but later Pat said that one of the things
that struck her deeply was the fact that as she and
Chappy left the track, they left to an applause
which generated when they first made it into the
public area, and lasted until they got into their car.

The following morning, when John
Hendrickson called on behalf of Mary Lou Whitney
to apologize for having won the race, he told Pat
that he and his wife were so sick over the victory
that they were unable to even sleep the night
before.

Mrs. Whitney later told Pat that she and John
Hendrickson had the only horse in the country that
was going to have to wear a bulletproof vest for the
rest of his career. At the time, Mrs. Whitney was
unaware that there had actually been an incident
after the race where one of the limo drivers who
was making a pickup in the barn area of the racetrack is alleged to have "taken a run" at their horse
with his car.

Prior to June 5, 2004, all of the things which had to go right, did. On June 5, 2004, Time Magazine had a reporter in the stands who had been hired to do the next edition's cover story, on Smarty Jones. When President Reagan died that morning, Bill Nack got a call on his cell phone. President Reagan was now the cover for the next edition.

The weather forecast was for rain. Not only did Smarty run well in the rain; Birdstone didn't. Birdstone had a dismal performance in the Kentucky Derby in the rain and had no interest in running on a "sealed track." Nick Zito admitted privately, that he and the Whitneys had already agreed that if "ONE DROP OF RAIN came down," Birdstone would be scratched and taken out of the race. An hour before the Belmont Stakes, the front that was brining the rain split in two. While the horses were approaching the starting gate, there was heavy rain to the east of the racetrack, and even heavier rain to the west of the facility. Zito had the paperwork in his jacket pocket which would withdraw Birdstone from the race before that "first drop of rain" hit the ground.

The rain never came, the paperwork remained in Zito's pocket, the two horses made their way into the starting gate, and the rest is history.

Smarty Jones didn't win this race, but his "split times" were all better than Secretariat in the Belmont Stakes which he won, resulting in his

Triple Crown. In THAT Belmont however, Secretariat only had one horse to beat...not three, in what amounted to three separate mini-races. Seattle Slew, another horse who Smarty had been oft compared to, didn't even have one other horse in his Belmont.

"The Kentucky Derby Gods have an agenda," another noted racing writer confided to me. "They pick out a good horse, with a great story, and make them both even better. The Triple Crown Gods are just mean."

In reflecting on the outcome of the Belmont, Sherry Servis told me, "We didn't know why our lives went down the road that they did. We didn't know why it was us to have won the Kentucky Derby, and the Preakness, or to have lost at Belmont. We just know that there was some pur- pose to all of it, and we went with the flow."

If life is at all a learning experience, perhaps the purpose of this series of races was to bring an absolutely amazing number of people together in support of the proposition that an individual can "win the big one" without even winning the big one.

The 2004 running of the Belmont Stakes was over, and once again, there would be no Triple Crown Winner. There would be more to be said about Smarty Jones however, and as usual, "Mr. Jones" would do much of that talking, for himself. Smarty Jones may have been beaten in the Belmont stakes and denied the Triple Crown, but he didn't "lose" anything, nor did anyone who was STILL along for the remainder of this ride.

CHAPTER THIRTEEN

REFLECTIONS

On the morning after Birdstone's victory in the Belmont, it was time for Smarty Jones to load into his van and head back to Philadelphia. Many of the same reporters who chronicled Smarty's journey from Philadelphia during the previous week were present for this departure, as well...but not all of them.

There was a police escort, one car this time... but no helicopters. The contingent of reporters who had followed in behind the motorcade earlier in the week were sound asleep, themselves dreaming of what might have been, and cursing the horse for having forced them to rewrite columns they had no doubt penned only days after the Preakness.

Fewer people honked, even fewer stopped in traffic...and while the locals would and did receive Smarty as the returning "Champion" that he most assuredly was, the van ride home was no different at all than the plane ride endured by every other Philly sports team who had come up just a bit short in the big game over the last twenty plus years.

It would have been easy for Smarty to mope out of that barn, hang his head and act as though his world had come to an end. After all, many of his biggest, most loyal and more passionate fans were still in shock regarding the events of the previous day. Had Smarty responded in that fashion, his actions would have been understood and easily accepted. But then...he wouldn't be Smarty.

On the morning after his defeat, this horse... this magnificent animal who had been so often compared to mythical champions like "Rocky," and the greatest in his sport, such as Secretariat and Seattle Slew, walked out of his stall with his head held high. Bill Foster remembers, "When Smarty walked out of the barn that morning, he made a move, not to the van, but toward the track. He wanted to get back on that track. He knew his work was not done."

As John recalls the experience, "Smarty came out and stopped where there were some reporters gathered, just like he always did. He waited for them to take their pictures, then he looked over toward the track, kinda nodded his head, and then trotted onto the van, just like he always did."

Throughout much of this work, I wanted to help the world understand how and why it is that people speak in terms of Smarty Jones as having a human-like persona. I asked another noted racing writer to tell me what it was, in his eyes that made Smarty different, in this respect. After contemplating the question for quite some time, he said finally, "I don't KNOW what it is; but, I always thought of him as a thinking, feeling, caring creature. When he lost, it was the first time in my life, professional or otherwise, that I ever actually felt sorry for a horse. I felt, for Smarty Jones, as I would feel FOR A PERSON, or a relative who had lost something...on a human level."

For two months, I asked people in Philadelphia, in California, in airports, in restaurants, hotels, and even several doctor's offices, retirement communities, and barber shops, all across the country, if they had heard of Smarty Jones, and if they had any thoughts on his brush with immortality. Once again, I was astonished that for an industry that many had suggested was on its' last legs not terribly long ago, the level of recognition, interest and understanding in connection with this animal was as broad-based and as far reaching as it quite clearly extends.

Everyone had heard of Smarty Jones.

Not only had they heard of him, but almost all of the more than 400 people that I spoke to actually DID remember "where they were" when "Smarty Jones lost the Triple Crown." Their stories were both heart-warming and gut-wrenching all at the same time. To a person, they could describe where they were, who they were with, and what their own thoughts were the moment each realized that Smarty was going to be passed.

Surprisingly, there were very, very few within this group whose immediate reaction was on the order of, "Oh no...looks like there won't be a Triple Crown winner again this year." By a wide margin, the feelings expressed were more of exactly the type and kind echoed by my writer friend, earlier. "That poor horse," many of them said...or, "he tried SO HARD." Many even suggested that "WE needed that SO BAD."

Many people "in racing" have and continue to suggest that "racing" needed, and needs a Triple Crown Winner. This may be true, for reasons relating to economic viability, if nothing else. However, the people I spoke to weren't "in racing" and they knew that America, and even the world needed not just "any" Triple Crown Winner...but THIS Triple Crown Winner. "We" didn't "need" Smarty to win in order to achieve any particular brand of stability, economic, emotional or otherwise. "We" needed THIS Triple Crown Winner because each and every one of us saw some part of ourselves...the good part...that we don't get a chance to remind ourselves about all that often, in Smarty Jones. We saw character. We saw values. We saw a work ethic. We saw heart, strength and at the same time grace, peace and beauty...inside and out.

A significant number of people in and out of the racing industry had suggested even before the Belmont Stakes that if Smarty Jones didn't win the Triple Crown, he would be "yesterday's news," and that no one would care about him any more.

After Smarty was defeated at Belmont, the amount of mail that he, John and the Chapmans were receiving DOUBLED. Three weeks after the Belmont, a dozen thoroughbred racehorses had their names officially changed, and mares in foal had names reserved for their foals which were ALL variations in one form or another of the name Smarty Jones.

Three months later, and after Smarty was officially retired, Sports Illustrated Magazine conducted a poll asking its' readership to identify the "sports personality" that they would most like to see make a comeback. This poll was taken at about the time that former NFL Star Running Back Ricky Williams was contemplating a return from exile... and seemed to be set up as a mechanism to garner public support in an effort to effect that return.

Ricky Williams was named in the poll results. But he finished SECOND in the balloting...to Smarty Jones.

Webster's Dictionary defines "personality" as, "the quality or state of being a person." Like my writer friend and the others I interviewed, apparently, at least 36% of the readership of a popular international sports magazine sees Smarty as something more than a horse, as well.

For over twenty years, the Commonwealth of Pennsylvania, or rather certain elements within the state, have been attempting to pass legislation expanding gambling within the state. When casino gambling came to New Jersey, and Delaware authorized slot machines at its' racetracks, Pennsylvania saw its' own race tracks begin to die a not so slow death, as well as tens of millions of tax dollars walking across one or the other of its' borders and into the coffers of neighboring states. Despite this fact, the pro-gaming lobby, and supportive legislators were substantially outnumbered by those within the state who wanted no part of any expansion of instate gambling.

After Smarty Jones won the second leg of the Triple Crown, and there were news reports which suggested that Smarty Jones might have to LEAVE Pennsylvania and move to another state, along with his trainer, because "Pennsylvania racetracks couldn't compete" from a prize money perspective with states where racetrack gaming was authorized...the state legislature extended a personal invitation to a horse trainer (John Servis) to make a special trip to Harrisburg, to explain why the legislature should forget about the last twenty years of haggling over the issue and get a gaming bill approved, NOW...before Smarty Jones moved elsewhere.

John accepted the invitation and provided testimony to the General Assembly regarding the need to have racing facilities authorized to install slot machines at their sites. THE VERY SAME DAY the legislature responded by forwarding a bill to the Governor which provided for in-state gaming, primarily at racetracks throughout the state.

Of course, as is usual in Pennsylvania, the legislature also saw fit to include a provision in the Bill authorizing each Member of the Legislature to actually own up to a one percent interest in any casino, but hey...they later bowed to public pressure on the issue of potential "conflict of interest" and a final Bill was signed by the Governor and is now law.

There WILL be casino gaming in the state of Pennsylvania, not because Harrah's has spent MILLIONS for the last twenty years, along with many other national gaming outlets, in order to attempt to expand their operations in Pennsylvania.

There WILL be casino gaming in Pennsylvania, because of Smarty Jones.

I wonder if any of those legislators stopped to

think that by the time ANY bill they might pass would become law and ultimately generate so much as a single dollar to make Pennsylvania Racetracks "more competitive," that Smarty Jones would be on about his third or fourth year of making new Little Smarties? I also wonder why in the face of problems even more obvious than preventing a racehorse from leaving the state, legislation can take years to pass, if it ever does get passed yet in this instance a mountain was moved in far less than even a twenty-four hour period...but that's another story.

I say this just to remind the first-ever winner-to-be of the first million dollar progressive slot machine jackpot in Pennsylvania about five years from now, to PLEASE remember to address your note of thanks, not to the Governor, not to the President of the State Senate, or any one of the Members of the Legislature (who may or may not own a one percent interest in the company who made the slot machine), but to send your thank you to a horse, who by that time, would have been living on a farm in Kentucky and already have "LEFT THE STATE" anyway.

In connection with some of the racing writers who took so long to get onto the Smarty Bandwagon in the first place, I am somewhat surprised, yet not surprised at all, by their willingness to be the first, and really the ONLY group to cast this great Champion aside, as though their own livelihoods DIDN'T depend on it.

At the time of this writing, balloting has recently concluded in connection with 2004 Eclipse Awards. Smarty Jones was eligible and nominated in two award categories, Three Year Old Champion, and 2004 Horse of the Year.

In connection with Horse of the Year Honors, Pre-balloting polls released a month ago suggested that Smarty Jones had "no shot" at winning Horse of the Year Honors. This despite the fact that as we already know, because John Servis said it many times, "all this horse did was win." A month later, the foregone became the conclusion, when the Eclipse Awards were presented...and Smarty was named Three Year Old Champion by a near unanimous vote, but at the same time denied the title of Horse of the Year.

Here was a horse who had come back from a tragic accident, and had no business being on a racetrack perhaps, at ALL. Not only did he return to racing, but he beat all comers, in eight out of eight races, and made himself available to run against the best of the best of the best, under circumstances where he had no more then three weeks between any race that he ran throughout the entire 2004 racing season.

In his first eight races, Smarty Jones won EIGHT TIMES, at EIGHT DIFFERENT DISTANCES, at FIVE DIFFERENT RACING FACILITIES, and as part of a schedule that no other horse even attempted to maintain. The horse he was narrowly defeated by, Birdstone, skipped the Preakness, and took five full weeks to prepare for Belmont after having his hat handed to him by Smarty Jones in the Kentucky Derby.

As was mentioned, six of the last eight racing seasons have seen the winner of the Kentucky Derby and Preakness also lose the Belmont. Not one of these horses did, for racing, sports in general, or the world at large...ANYTHING like was given to that entire collection of entities, in the manner of benefit which was given freely by this year's Triple Crown Contender. Likewise, no "Horse of the Year" for any one of those years, or for perhaps ANY year, brought more new blood to the racing industry, or more interest, acclaim and praise to the same industry and everyone in it...than did Smarty Jones. In fact...try this Pepsi Challenge, on for size...If you are not a voter for this award, NAME ANY ONE of the last eight "Horses of the Year," please.

The 2004 "insider's choice" for "Horse of the Year" was a horse who raced only four times this season, as part of a carefully crafted schedule which included significant periods of inactivity. This, notwithstanding the fact that one of the knocks on Smarty was that he "didn't race enough" to win the award.

While Horse of the Year may not appropriately be a popularity contest, perhaps in this instance, voting should have been opened up to the fans.

Smarty Jones was directly responsible for the record crowds at this year's Triple Crown Races, and for the record wagering on those races, and for the fact that for the first time in history, the Belmont Stakes was not only the highest rated telecast of the day, but also for the MONTH in which it aired. The Last Belmont to rate higher in raw numbers than 2004; 1977...when Seattle Slew won the Triple Crown.

My point is rather simple in this respect. Nine months ago, I would have considered myself a racing fan. I watch the big races every year. I have been to racetracks off and on throughout the course of my adult life. I had never taken any one of my children to a racetrack, nor had any one of them asked to go, until now...until Smarty Jones.

We are a nation which is steeped in great tradition. The sad fact, however, is that many of those traditions; things that were held near and dear in many cases, a century ago or longer, are dying out, or have already had the plug pulled on them. Pick a city, or a state, in any region of the country, and you can find things that used to be that are no more. Great Grandparents, Grandparents, and in some cases even our parents tell us about things they "always" USED to do, or places they always USED to go. One ritual after another, one favorite pastime after another has...and others undoubtedly will continue to "go by the wayside."

How many Elks Clubs are left in the country? Philadelphia's own "Mummer's Parade" which for a hundred years drew more a million people to stand in sub-zero temperatures for a full day every January 1st, is a shadow of its former self, and may one day be gone. A significant portion of the event has already begun to be held at an indoor facility in front of a far more limited number of spectators.

Every major college football bowl game USED to have lavish parades which drew significant television ratings. Now but for a few exceptions, networks can't give away the ad time, and only carry the parade, if it even continues to exist, as part of a package to get the football game.

Racetracks are not OPENING all across the country. In point of fact, there are many more which are closing or in financial trouble, than are opening. The only racetrack expansion in America, is taking place in locations where the expansion relates to the addition of casino operations.

So, along comes a horse who captures the hearts, minds, souls, AND LOYALTIES...NOT JUST OF ITS' DYING FAN BASE...but of CHILDREN... CHILDREN who are the next generation fan base, and who might keep the industry from being reduced to the significance of the Calabasas Frog Jumping Contest (no offense to the frogs, or Calabasas), and the thank you to be received by a horse who outpolls humans in a contest dealing with sports "personalities" is to dishonor him by withholding an award which has been received by not a "Who's Who," but a "WHO WAS THAT" band of now namelss, faceless, PERSONALITY-LESS predecessors who have accomplished FAR less than has he?

Perhaps this is why Sally Marshall, a 63 year

old woman from Eagan, Minnesota who was not a racing fan prior to 2004 had organized a national fan effort in support of Smarty Jones as 2004 Horse of the Year.

More than one voter remarked privately that the vote for Smarty as Three Year Old Champion was a vote FOR the horse, but that withholding the Horse of the Year vote was actually a vote against Smarty's Owners and what these voters perceived as Smarty's "early retirement."

Having spent hours upon hours interviewing virtually everyone associated with Team Smarty, I can safely say that NO ONE wanted to see this horse run, even ONE MORE TIME...more than this group.

Over 370,000 people attended the three Triple Crown Races in 2004 in person. Tens of millions more watched the races on worldewide television. These people named Smarty Jones "2004 Horse of the Year" with the way they responded to this great champion, before and after his only defeat.

Less than 300 people stripped him of that title, in large part over a dispute regarding the decision to retire the horse...and to at least some extent, just because they could.

While I find it an abomination to all that Smarty Jones stood for...for a group of less than three hundred people to the deny the title of Horse of the Year to perhaps the sport's ALL-TIME worthiest non-recipient, I also understand any fan, and any voter's frustration with not seeing Smarty race again, because that same frustration is shared by everyone who was an intimate part of the Smarty Jones Story.

Fans, including those with a vote in this poll, gave there hearts and souls to this horse, every time he stepped on the track. We didn't just "watch" Smarty, we LIVED him. We WERE Stewart Elliott, or John Servis, or Pat Chapman. Some of us were even Bill Foster and Roy Chapman. We just wanted to be more of a part of something so special as to captivate virtually every age group in every corner of the world.

When Smarty raced at Belmont, none of us knew it would be his final race. None of us had a chance to prepare for the fact that someone who had become so much a part of so many of our lives, would never perform for us again.

Cher had a farewell tour. Michael Jordan had three or four. In this day and age, no major entertainment or "sports personality" rides off into the sunset without one. There was a time when I thought, why do you need a farewell tour...just retire already, will ya? But, as previously noted, our world is changing.

Smarty gave a great deal to us over the course of his albeit brief racing career. Like the writer who wasn't sure why he felt the way he did about Smarty...I honestly can't explain how Smarty Jones captured the hearts that he did around the world, or why it was him, as opposed to Rock Hard Ten. Heck, they both have nice names. There was something about Smarty Jones. He had a marvelously inspiring story behind him. He had owners that were hard working, blue collar, salt of the earth people. He had a trainer who there aren't enough five star adjectives to describe or enough glowing terms to utilize. He had a FAMILY! And, they invited us in...to be a part of that family...and as a WORLD, we invited them right back, into OUR family.

Wherever you were when you were watching Smarty Jones race, everything was right in the world. It didn't matter if you were at a private home or a racetrack, an airport lounge or even a bus station. The age, race, sex, political affiliation or outlook on life of the person standing next to you was of no consequence.

In a world which is literally more at war than the vast majority of us can begin to realize; in a nation where we can't find so much as a single issue that even a mere majority of us can agree on, let ALONE "rally around"...in an era where virtually nothing is certain; we were finally blessed with the presence of an individual/animal/personality (take your pick) where there WAS certainty.

Smarty would give the world awe inspiring performances, each and every time he stepped on a racetrack, and in his own way demonstrate to "the higher species" that if we truly believed and worked not just hard, but harder than we thought we were capable of, we could do anything.

He gave us hope.

He gave an 11 year old boy in Captiva, Florida with a rare muscular-skeletal disease, hope. He gave the mother of a sick dog in Houston Texas, hope. He gave a little girl in Arizona with eye problems of her own, hope. He gave us something to rally around as a nation for the first time in years.

And, he made us forget.

He made us forget about people trying to harm us. He made us forget about soldiers dying, oil prices rising, prescription drug costs, corporate scandals, celebrity murder trials, the war on drugs, the war on crime, or who may or may not be appointed to the Supreme Court.

Smarty Jones made us remember, too.

He made us remember back to a time in our lives when things were simple...when the only thing that mattered was who won a horse race. He didn't care about where he came from. He didn't run for the money. His owners didn't run him for the money. His trainer didn't train him for the money, or hold him out of the Preakness because he wanted a bigger piece of the pie. Smarty Jones made us remember back to a time when it was the GAME that mattered...NOT the player.

Most importantly, for most of us; Smarty Jones did what we ask our parents to do. He did what we ask whoever our God is, to do. He did what we ask those who love us, to do...and what we try to do for those that we love.

Smarty Jones made all of the bad things go away.

And, when I reflect on the entire experience, I can understand why some of the racing writers feel put out by Smarty's "early" retirement.

I can also understand why Smarty's new home has had to hire a Public Relations Coordinator, expand the size of their parking lot, and operate two tours per day which are booked months in advance, just so people can come and visit Smarty Jones.

I can understand why the Gehrke family of Wisconsin, the Trull family from Nevada, the Woodwards of Texas, and the Holan family of Illinois, along with tens of thousands of others are all planning to take this year's family vacations in Midway, Kentucky.

When Smarty Jones was passed by Birdstone in the final ten seconds of the 2004 Belmont Stakes, not a single person who was present or who watched that race on television, thought that this would be the last time they would that they would ever witness this great thoroughbred run.

On nine different occasions over the previous seven months, Smarty Jones had given absolutely everything that he could muster from within himself...to US. Unless Smarty Jones really IS a human being, with the capacity to feel, and to appreciate, and to understand as only a human can...Smarty Jones did what he did, FOR OUR BENEFIT! Every time he reached deep down for an extra burst of speed, he did it for US.

And, while the baseball player who takes illegal steroids so he can get a better contract, or the basketball player who only gives his best during the playoffs, or the football player who tells a certain team not to draft him because he won't play there, will all ultimately finish their careers and have an entire season which will serve as their "Farewell Tour," Smarty Jones gave ten times the effort of any of these other athletes...and HE did it, FOR US.

Nine races, eight wins, the thrill of victory, the agony of defeat, the declaration of hero status, the installation as a true cultural icon...and then it was over; with none of us having so much as an opportunity to even say "goodbye."

When Maureen Donnelly saw Smarty Jones run for the first time, she screamed, "At last, someone was right in their assessment of a horse."

When Smarty Jones was gone, I screamed, "I GET IT! Now I know why REAL STARS need a farewell tour."

Smarty gave, and gave, and gave to us; and we gladly took...because as in the case of every great athlete, neither the athlete, nor the fans really ever believe there will be an end. And, on that day, when it does end...or at least shortly before; we will most assuredly all have a chance to say good-bye...to say thank you...to give back.

We got none of that in the case of this great athlete. We thought we would. We expected that we would. And, since very few people could even accept that Smarty Jones had actually been beaten...how could we possibly expect to simply be able to let go, without even so much as having an opportunity to say "goodbye?"

Smarty's racing career was guided by very intelligent, very horse savvy, very caring and compassionate people, NONE of whom would have done a single thing to harm this animal in any way. After the Kentucky Derby, John Servis would not even commit to running in the Preakness until after he was convinced that Smarty was ready to go, and didn't need a break. When Smarty injured himself in that starting gate, the Chapmans insured that he received care at one of the world's most respected equine medical facilities, from a veterinarian who has substantially more people desiring her services, than hours in the day will allow her to accept.

The decision to retire Smarty Jones was arrived at after consultation with a number of the world's most noted and recognized equine medical professionals; and further consultation with the horse's training staff...and it was not only the proper decision, but the only decision which could have been made. It was clearly and entirely based upon questions of care, compassion and concern for Smarty Jones, as well as his short and long-term health and best interests...made by people who absolutely had and still have those interests at the height of their consideration.

Some racing writers claim Smarty Jones shouldn't have been retired. In this regard however, they have no evidence to support their claim...certainly no competent veterinary medical evidence and discount the efforts made by Team Smarty to provide for the safety and security of Smarty Jones. It wasn't only Smarty Jones and those around him who considered him human-like, if not in fact a human being. Roy and Pat Chapman considered him no less than their sixth child. Their decisions regarding medical treatment, course of proceeding and the election to retire Smarty was one that while certain of those within the racing industry were loathe to accept...was the only decision any parent could EVER make.

Millions of fans simply can't believe that their hero is gone, under circumstances where they had no chance to give him back any of the emotion or passion that he shared with them over the course of his brief but illustrious career.

Ironically, in the end the writers and the fans are both saying the same thing in different ways. They didn't get enough Smarty Jones, and they want more.

John Servis and numerous others clearly

understood that at some point in time, Smarty Jones stopped being Bensalem's Horse and became first America's Horse...and ultimately the World's Horse. While it was a wonderful thing to have Smarty take a "Victory Lap" in front of an overflow crowd back at Philadelphia Park and call it a "Retirement Ceremony," it was clearly no way for this great champion to bid farewell to an entire world which had placed him in a position of great honor, esteem and regard.

Imagine a parade in honor of the 2004 World Series Champion Boston Red Sox...and the Red Sox didn't show up. Imagine being a small boy and being told that the last in the series of your favorite comic book would come out in a month, and you waited, and waited, and waited...but the last issue was never printed. Imagine a horse who had captured the hearts and souls of an entire worldwide generation of people...and he just went away.

Yes, Smarty Jones needed to retire. Neither he, nor his owners or handlers, or anyone who participated in making this decision should be frowned upon or punished in any way for the hand that was dealt by the Powers That Be.

Neither should one of the greatest competitors in the history of this sport.

His many legions of fans also needed an opportunity to thank Smarty Jones...to give back to him what he gave to us; and to give him our love, as we said "goodbye." It was only natural for all who felt so included, and that they were so much a part of the rest of the ride, to also feel so left out, when their hero just went away.

Those who are physically and financially able to do so, will go to Midway, Kentucky at some time, and say their private and very personal thank yous to Smarty Jones for the manner in which he was able to touch and inspire them. Far more will be left only with the memory of his having been passed by a horse whose name they can't remember, in the final ten seconds of the Belmont Stakes

.

THOSE fans deserve better, and so does Smarty Jones.

CHAPTER FOURTEEN

WHAT IS A CHAMPION?

Each year, every amateur and professional sports organization, league or governing body will declare a new "Champion". The world craves "Champions". The vast majority of the world aspires to one day, BE a "Champion," of something; or anything ...and in lieu of being a "Champion," is more than happy to participate in some way in the crowning of someone else, as a "Champion."

Today, if you look hard enough, you can find champions in categories including everything from bass fishing to hog calling; from "yelling" to spelling bees. If none of these particular champions suits your personal agenda, or should you seek to identify a champion in any category which has yet to declare one...you can rest assured that the newest cable network with no programming will be happy to schedule the *World's Strongest Man Who Can Fill The Most Cream Donuts Manually While Playing Texas Hold-Em Poker, Barrels Racing AND Running a Triathlon All At the Same Time* National or World Championship...just for you.

So, in a world where you can't swing a dead cat without hitting at least two, maybe three HUNDRED "Champions"...what IS a "Champion?"

A Champion is not just an individual that we as a society strive to become, or even to simply to "be like." A Champion inspires us. Champions stimulate us. They bring us to a renewed belief in all things possible, restore our faith in ourselves, our faith in each other and even cultivate the concept of faith, generally. In this sense a champion is some combination of philosopher, theologian and perhaps magician. Champions are also artists...masters of their own form of canvas. They paint a present day picture which can be seen only through their eyes...and then they share that present day picture, in the form of a road map which becomes our collective vision for what we hope our own future might look like.

Personally, I smile when I realize that most people honestly do understand that it wasn't five NBA Championship Rings which made Michael Jordan a Champion, or drew people to want to "be like" him.

The true beauty associated with the concept of being a champion lies in the fact that champions will come in all forms, in and out of a sports context or setting. The bittersweet reality however remains while the average person is locked in many instances, in a never-ending quest to identify a field within which they may achieve some commercially recognizable version of champion status...attainment of this particular goal is rarely forthcoming. Champions are special people not because anyone can become one, even in this day and age of the vast abuse of the term, but because true champions in ny setting are in FACT, still a very rare breed.

We ARE "ALL Champions" in one sense. Any time that we open ourselves up to the inspiration of a true champion and the result is that we work harder, run faster, jump higher or simply do something differently in our lives than we have ever done before...we have taken on at least a single quality of that true champion. Once again, however, there is a significant difference between this inspiration itself, and the inspired.

Of the thousands of new Champions who are crowned each year in one form or another, ALL were in some way "inspired." Few if any will cause you or I to do even that one single thing differently in our own lives, today, tomorrow, or ever.

When the Great American Patriot, Patrick Henry delivered a speech to the Second Virginia Convention on March 20, 1775, and proudly proclaimed, "Give me liberty, or give me death," HE was a Champion. Likewise, when twenty-one year old Nathan Hale was about to be hanged by the British on September 22, 1776 after advising his captors, "I regret that I have but one life to lose for my country," HE was a Champion.

When Eli Whitney, George Washington Carver, Louie Pasteur, Albert Einstein, Dr. Christian Barnard, Abraham Lincoln, Martin Luther King, John Kennedy and yes, even Bill Gates, refused to walk away from the missions which had been given them, as each had a free will opportunity to so do; and instead gave of themselves so that entire generations of people might live and live more productively, and peacefully, and in some way DIFFERENT than absent the contribution of these individuals... THEY were ALL Champions.

Confining ourselves for the moment to the arena in which all sports are witnessed; by the time the average individual reaches the age of five, he or she customarily has a "favorite" sport and/or player and might even want mom or dad to go to a game, buy a jersey, secure an autograph, or something else along those lines. At that game, if the novelty stand is out of one jersey, another will usually do. Few fans turn down autographs even of athletes they don't recognize; and win or lose there is little chance that anything will happen in today's game that will alter the course of history in that sport, in society in general, or cause any spectator to have a different day, tomorrow, than they had today.

Due to the fact that in most instances, time really does march on; the same individual who asked mom and dad to go to a sporting event at the age of five, could one day have a five year old of his or her own. Even absent the pitter-patter of little feet, our "inspired" will ultimately reflect back upon their own sporting experience at some point during their adult life, recalling those events and moments which brought them great joy.

In my own life, you could pick a sport and my greatest memory from that sport would likely begin with me saying, "I never saw Babe Ruth, play," or, "I remember Wilt Chamberlain, but never saw him play, either." I missed the great runs that people tell me were made by Jim Brown, and Gale Sayers. I don't really remember Mickey Mantle or Bill Russell. I skated with Gordie Howe...but I was thirty, and quite possibly, THIS great Champion was a stone's throw from the century mark. I wasn't there when Roger Bannister broke the four minute mile. I wasn't paying attention when Billie Jean King changed the game of tennis, and while I remember Secretariat barreling down the home stretch at Belmont Park on the way to the Triple Crown and looking like he was the only horse in the race, it didn't cause me to spend the next afternoon "riding on a pony."

I DO remember OJ Simpson's 2000 yard rushing season...even the part where in the last game, while he was attempting to be the first to eclipse the 2000 yard mark, the official game statistician on at least one occasion went back and added a yard here and a yard there to runs that had already taken place, apparently in an effort to make sure that history was made that afternoon.

I also remember the destruction of OJ Simpson, basketball brawls, hockey players jailed for conspiring to murder their agents, a member of the only ever 16-0 NFL team serving time in a federal prison for drug trafficking, Little League World Series players being disqualified and adult coaches being banned for life for cheating at the proverbial "child's game," the greatest all-around baseball player in the history of the game banned from baseball and made ineligible for post-career honors, one sports sex scandal after another, questions arising regarding each and every major league baseball power hitting record, due to the alleged, or in at least a few cases admitted use of steroids...and a mad rush to add the proverbial asterisk (*) to so many different records in so many different sports as to turn the average sports history museum into at least a Hall of Fame* if not a Hall of Shame.

In fact, with estimates as high as the mid-thirty percent range suggesting athletes at the high school level AND BELOW have or are taking ILLEGAL performance enhancing drugs IN THE HOPE OF BECOMING "Champions," there is an ever increasing lobby in this country and around the world seeking to redirect dedicated school sports funding to other, more "academic pursuits."

This is usually about the time that a TRUE Champion emerges to help the rest of us all remember what Champions are, why we revere them, why we are compelled to live our lives through them, and why we change the way we do things because of them.

Thank you, Pat Tillman.

Thank you, Curt Schilling.

Thank you, Lance Armstrong.

Thank you, Tiger Woods.

Thank you, Arthur Ashe and Jim Valvano; your work lives on.

Thank you, Mia Hamm

Thank you, Venus and Serena Williams

THANK YOU, SMARTY JONES!

On behalf of the great "inspired" worldwide, "thank you." You have all changed, and continue to change your games, and the lives in general of all who have witnessed your play.

As a young person, seeing Secretariat win a Triple Crown was electric. As an adult, seeing Smarty Jones passed by a 36-1 longshot with seventy yards between Smarty and his own Triple Crown, I was moved...as were the 100,000+ in the stands, and the tens of millions who were left in a puddle of grief, disbelief and astonishment.

Secretariat's triumph was most assuredly a great moment in racing. The moments that we ALL shared with Smarty Jones, before, during and after the 2004 Belmont Stakes TRANSCENDED racing.

By the time Smarty left Philadelphia, for Arkansas, he had a fan base. When he left Arkansas, he was already a local folk hero. After the Kentucky Derby, he was already "America's Champion." Smarty had already changed a number of lives as the result of his efforts, and already, legions of followers were altering their daily life rituals and routines for any one of a number of reasons. Some wanted to be a larger part of what was happening in Smarty's world. Others drew strength and inspiration from his story and applied that strength to their own lives. Many simply wanted to "be like Smarty."

After Smarty's victory in the Preakness, the foreign press, already on the Smarty Bandwagon as a group anyway, proclaimed his greatness to all who would listen in every corner of the world.

Congratulations, Smarty Jones, you are now a true cultural phenomenon, societal icon, sports hero and a step away, in the minds of many, from immortality. You are also a "Champion." You have been declared a Champion, eight times; and have the pictures from eight Winner's Circles to prove it.

So...what IS "a Champion?"

Webster's Dictionary defines "Champion" in the following manner:
"1: WARRIOR, FIGHTER
2: a militant advocate or defender
<a champion of civil rights>
3: one that does battle for another's rights or honor <God will raise me up A champion. Sir Walter Scott>
4: a winner of first prize or first place in a competition.

In September 2004, 36%, presumably all of whom were at least in part members of a species known as human beings, voted Smarty Jones the "Sports Personality" they would most like to see make a comeback.

In December 2004, Smarty Jones was named as a finalist for an award known as the Most Inspiring PERSON of 2004, as presented by Beliefnet.com. In attempting to explain at length, how an animal ended up on a list of candidates for the Most Inspiring PERSON of 2004, the editors at Beliefnet suggested that Smarty Jones had inspired millions, and served as "a powerful antidote to troubled times." The commentary went on to discuss Smarty's courage, and power...his racing ability, the impact he had on children, at home and around the world, and even borrowed a line from a letter written by Beach Cutler, an 11 year old boy from Captiva, FL with serious physical difficulties. To Beach Cutler, and now to the staff at Beliefnet.,

Smarty Jones had become, "an icon of hope."

Smarty's Beliefnet profile concluded with the following passage:

"We identified with his struggles, exulted in his triumphs and recognized the heartbreak of his loss. We flew away with Smarty Jones, asking him to outrun the world's imperfections and carry our hope beyond the limits of humanity."

The list of Finalists for the Beliefnet.com honor as Most Inspiring PERSON of 2004 included the likes of Pat Tillman, Christopher Reeve and Nancy Reagan. In fact, while Smarty didn't win the Award; that honor was afforded to the Late Christopher Reeve, he DID actually receive more votes than Mrs. Reagan, and several of the others from among the group of Finalists.

At about the same time, Time Magazine announced not only its' famed "Person of the Year," but also its' list of "PEOPLE Who Mattered in 2004." Only four names appear from among the group of Finalists for the Beliefnet.com Most Inspiring PERSON Award...Pat Tillman, Lance Armstrong, Christopher Reeve; and Smarty Jones.

The Time list also includes the likes of Ronald Reagan, Israeli Prime Minister Ariel Sharon, Afghan President Hamid Karzai, Ukrainian President Victor Yuschenko, Iraqi Interim Leader Ilyad Alawi, Presidential Candidate John Kerry, Steve Jobs - Corporate Baron, and New York Attorney General, Eliot Spitser.

Time's profile cited Smarty's race for the

Triple Crown and called it, "the year's most captivating race (aside from the one for the White House)..."

As I reviewed these, and a series of other end of year awards, all of which Smarty was a Finalist for, and all of which were designed and intended for actual "PERSONS," I was finally struck by the most significant fact associated with what was happening at this time.

It wasn't simply that Smarty Jones was being placed on lists of "Most Inspiring People," or "Persons Who Mattered." The single most amazing aspect of this entire story lies in the fact that NOT ONLY, did WE, as a worldwide community of PEOPLE...NOT THINK TWICE, about including a horse on list after list honoring PERSONS and PEOPLE, but that ONCE ON the list...IT WAS AS NATURAL FOR ANY OF US TO CAST A VOTE FOR SMARTY JONES, as it was to cast a vote for Ronald Reagan, Nancy Reagan, or Hamid Karzai.

Reasoned, rational, logical people who OFFER these prizes didn't bat an eye about placing Smarty on the list, and the rest of the world was more than a little bit comfortable in voting for him.

In the Beliefnet.com Poll, one person was actually OFFENDED that Pat Tillman's name even appeared on the list. Pat Tillman, as you recall was the NFL Member of the Arizona Cardinals who left a lucrative and promising NFL career to enlist in the military, and who was later killed in action in Afghanistan. The individual who was offended at his

inclusion on the list was concerned that news outlets had allegedly reported that Pat Tillman was "a
devout atheist" and as such was not properly
includable on a list of inspiring people generated by
the editors of a spiritually-based website.

On the other hand, IT DIDN'T SEEM TO MAT-
TER THAT THE SAME PERSON CONCERNED
ABOUT ONE CANDIDATE BEING AN ATHEIST and
becoming the Most Inspiring Person of 2004...WAS
not at ALL troubled by HIS OWN SUPPORT FOR A
HORSE to win that same award. The Quaker in me
recognizes that there is NO WAY that Smarty Jones
came, or did what he did, as the result of mere hap-
penstance. However, to suggest that A HORSE,
could be more "SPIRITUALLY SOUND" than ANY
HUMAN, regardless of that human's thought
process, is what makes this story, this book, this
experience, and Smarty Jones...different.

In defining a "Champion" Webster CLEARLY
placed the least possible emphasis on actually "winning" any award. Webster's definition of a
"Champion" squarely places the primary qualifying
criteria EXACTLY where it should be...on the
CHARACTER of an individual.

"Warrior...Fighter?" Not even the most ardent
detractor could make the claim that Smarty Jones
was anything BUT one of the fiercest competitors
that the sport of horse racing, or ANY sport, has
EVER witnessed.

"Militant advocate...Defender of the right's of
another?" Dee Brophy Herrling said it best in her

own letter written directly to "Mr. Smarty Jones," when she said, "You ran for all of us who came from the wrong side of the tracks." Dee's letter was one of more than a million letters which came in from across the United States and around the world, each in their own way wanting, telling, NEEDING Smarty Jones, to KNOW...that THEY KNEW...he was doing all that he was doing, NOT FOR HIMSELF, and not even for his owners, trainers, and handlers; but that he was doing it all for THEM...whether Smarty Jones even appreciated that fact or not. That these authors collectively attributed TO Smarty Jones, the CAPACITY to appreciate that fact, is what MAKES Smarty Jones the "Champion" that he has become.

The fact that following the Belmont Stakes; and at a time when as a species, WE HUMANS find it MORE than natural to cast aside anyone who is not "getting their picture taken" as we bark out "what have you done for me lately" in seven different languages...and that in this instance the popularity and praise for this hero multiplied exponentially...is what has KEPT Smarty Jones a "Champion."

I asked one person if he felt any differently about Smarty Jones after the Belmont Stakes, as opposed to the day before. He told me, "Before OR after Belmont, the name, Smarty Jones still has the same magical sound to it...you know, Jones...Smarty Jones. Just like Bond... James Bond."

I asked a member of the New York Media, the

day after the 2004 Belmont, to explain why on the morning after the death of one of the perceived greatest Presidents in the history of our nation, a horse's photo and story appeared across the top of the front page of the New York Times. The response, "Smarty touched a broader BASE of people," even than that former President.

Smarty Jones was "A winner of first prize or first place in a competition," eight times as a matter of fact; but no one, any combination, or all of those wins, made him a "Champion." And, when you really think about it; Smarty Jones didn't LOSE anything, even at Belmont...he just came in second.

It is the life and times of Smarty Jones, the CHARACTER displayed by this animal, and the inspiration that he gave, and continues to give tens of millions of people on an otherwise troubled planet that has made him not only a Champion for today, but that has made him, "Forever a Champion."

There will be other great athletes in all of sport, horse racing included. There will be world leaders whose contribution to society will warrant their inclusion on lists of those who inspire, or who mattered, or who should be remembered. There will be new lists created, new champions crowned, more scandal and controversy in and out of sports. But there will never be another human, animal, or member of a species yet to be identified; into whose eyes ANY person will look, and see the purity, and inspiration, and RAW GOODLINESS, and innocence of purpose which are present in the heart and soul of this "warrior"...this "fighter"...this militant advocate in defense of others.

There will never be another Smarty Jones; and because these memories will last more than a lifetime...that's okay, too.

Thank you, Smarty Jones. You ARE...

"Forever a Champion."